# Markt- und Unternehmensentwicklung / Markets and Organisations

**Edited by**
A. Picot, München, Germany
R. Reichwald, Leipzig, Germany
E. Franck, Zürich, Switzerland
K. M. Möslein, Erlangen-Nürnberg, Germany

Change of institutions, technology and competition drives the interplay of markets and organisations. The scientific series 'Markets and Organisations' addresses a magnitude of related questions, presents theoretic and empirical findings and discusses related concepts and models.

Vivek K. Velamuri

# Hybrid Value Creation

Springer Gabler

Vivek K. Velamuri
HHL Leipzig Graduate School of Management
Leipzig, Germany

Dissertation Friedrich-Alexander-Universität Erlangen-Nürnberg, 2011

ISBN 978-3-8349-3960-9 ISBN 978-3-8349-3961-6 (eBook)
DOI 10.1007/978-3-8349-3961-6

The Deutsche Nationalbibliothek lists this publication in the Deutsche Nationalbibliografie; detailed bibliographic data are available in the Internet at http://dnb.d-nb.de.

Library of Congress Control Number: 2013933368

Springer Gabler


Printed on acid-free paper

Springer Gabler is a brand of Springer DE.
Springer DE is part of Springer Science+Business Media.
www.springer-gabler.de

*All my life I've had doubts about who I am, where I belonged.*
*Now I'm like the arrow that springs from the bow.*
*No hesitation, no doubts.*
*The path is clear.*

*– Sinclair*

# Foreword

Hybrid value creation - a phenomenon also known under different terms such as *"Product Service Systems"*, *"Dematerialization"*, and *"Servitization"* - triggers the fundamental transformation of individual firms and whole economies. While in the last 20 years it has mainly been firms in the western industrialized economies who have engaged in the process of generating additional value by innovatively combining products (tangible component) and services (intangible component), the phenomenon has recently gained speed in emerging markets. As Vivek Velamuri convincingly argues, hybrid value creation is highly attractive for firms for the following reasons (1) *economic:* as substantial revenue can be generated, (2) *strategic:* as firms can gain a competitive advantage that is difficult to imitate, (3) *environmental:* as the same economic function can be served with a reduction in the quantity of materials required in doing so, and (4) *innovation:* as radically new offerings or business models can be created. Overall, the thesis at hand is comprehensive in its approach and reveals results that are not only of high interest for academia, but also extremely insightful for business practice.

First, by conducting a systematic literature review, the author provides an impressive state-of-the-art report. Next, using a deductive analysis of 80 case vignettes, four distinct clusters of hybrid value creation are developed: embedded products, leasing/ renting/ sharing/ pooling, mass customization, and solutions. Finally, in-depth cases from global players such as Adidas, Electrolux, Siemens, and Viessmann reveal credible success factors for the clusters of embedded products as well as solutions. In total, this dissertation provides a systematic assessment of the state-of-the-art of the field and identifies empirically derived strategies for hybrid value creation across different industrial sectors. Also with specific industry examples the author helps the reader to follow the research with ease.

I personally congratulate Vivek Velamuri on the impressive result of his doctoral research and recommend the book to management researchers and practitioners alike. The dissertation has already been nominated to the 2011 Industry Studies Association (ISA) best dissertation award. I am looking forward to future results in this important research stream. All the best, Vivek, for your future academic career!

Prof. Dr. Kathrin M. Möslein

**Acknowledgement**

Anne SH

BB Basti

BMBF (Project Sprint, FKZ 01FD0610)

Carlos

Caro

Chris B.

Chrisi

dad

Dome

Dr. Neyer

Emilio

FAU

Geb CWS

Hari

KfP Jörg

Kathrin

Marga

mom

Meisengeige

NN Jens

Sabi

Sandra

Schrey

Schreyers

Stefan

Zimmer & Co.

-

Babsi (for keeping me grounded ...not that ...it was necessary)

# Overview of Contents

## V - Empirical Study 3 - The Cluster of Solutions



## VI - Discussion and Conclusion



## Annexes

# Table of Contents

## Part III - Empirical Study 1 - The Four Clusters of Hybrid Value Creation

# List of Figures

# List of Tables

# I

# Introduction: Setting the Stage

# 1 The Relevance of Hybrid Value Creation

*"Instead of selling airlines first engines and then parts and service, Rolls-Royce has convinced its customers to pay a fee for every hour that an engine runs. Rolls-Royce in turn promises to maintain it and replace it if it breaks down. 'They aren't selling engines, they are selling hot air out the back of an engine,' says an investment analyst."*

The Economist, *Jan 8, 2009*

It is increasingly recognized, as seen in the epigraph above, that more and more firms are shifting their focus from offering standalone products or services towards offering integrated combinations of products and services to better meet specific demands of customers (Araujo and Spring 2006; Davies 2004; Oliva and Kallenberg 2003; Tukker 2004; Windahl et al. 2004). The popularity of combining products and services, however, is not enough for such a strategy to be successful and to motivate firms to experiment with this phenomenon. It has to make economic sense, i.e., it has to create value that can be monetized. This process of creating value through combining products and services is known as hybrid value creation. It is defined as:

> *"the process of generating additional value by innovatively combining products (tangible component) and services (intangible component)".*

Creating value by selling "hot air out of the back of an engine" as in the case of Rolls-Royce is one possibility to engage in hybrid value creation. In other cases, products are not sold but rented or shared. For example, the business model of PoshBags4rent (www.poshbags4rent.de) revolves around renting designer handbags to customers for a short duration of time. By doing so, the firm expands its customer base by acquiring customers who cannot afford to buy a Louis Vuitton or Prada handbag, but who nevertheless would like to use one. Another exotic example of a renting business model is Flexpetz (www.flexpetz.com), which allows for the sharing of pet dogs between customers.

An alternate way of combining products and services is through providing customization services on a product. For example, MyMuesli (www.mymuesli.com) sells customized breakfast cereal, combining different ingredients to meet specific customer tastes, or Nike (www.nikeid.com) fabricates shoes to meet the exact design wishes of its customers.

One could also combine products and services by embedding services into the product using digital technologies. For example, Kindle (www.kindle.com), the eBook reader provided by Amazon, allows for the purchase and download of eBooks from the online store. Whereas, the adidas's miCoach (www.micoach.com) offers a real-time training system designed to motivate, inspire, and enable athletes at all levels to reach their training goals. Its advanced interactive training system collects and turns personal data into individual training plans based on one's fitness level and specific goals.

Finally, products and services can be seamlessly combined into a solution that allows the customer to focus on their core competencies. As seen in the Rolls-Royce (www.rolls-royce.com) example, the firm takes over responsibility for the engines. In fact, it charges the customer a fixed engine maintenance cost over an extended time period. In other words, through its trademarked *'power-by-the-hour'* business model, the firm, in effect, charges its customer for every minute an engine is running. Similarly, Hilti (www.hilti.com) provides a total tool fleet management solution to its customer. For this, the firm charges a fixed amount and in return takes over responsibility for managing the construction tools its customers require. Thereby, the firm helps its customers focus on managing their core business of construction.

Looking at all the above-mentioned examples, it becomes amply clear that there are many unique ways that firms can combine products and services. It is also clear that the phenomenon of combining products and services is not limited to a handful of industries, but covers various sectors. Extant research has identified that the phenomenon of hybrid value creation is visible in a diverse range of industries and sectors from automotive, building, chemical, white goods, and electronic to the food industry (Goedkoop et al. 1999; Rocchi 2005). Also, product–service combinations can range from simple delivery services or fixed price per copy solutions provided by Xerox, Ricoh, Océ, and Hewlett Packard (Rocchi 2005) to complex turnkey products such as the design, construction, and operation of mobile networks as in the case of Ericsson Mobile Communication Systems (Brady, Davies, and Gann 2005a). These product-service combinations are relevant in both business-to-business (b2b) and business-to-customer (b2c) markets (Mont 2004a).

Moving to the arguments underpinning the increasing popularity of such product-service offerings in today's business environment, Oliva and Kallenberg (2003) suggest that all arguments can be broadly clustered into:

1. *Economic:* as substantial revenue can be generated,
2. *Strategic:* as firms can gain a competitive advantage that is difficult to imitate, and
3. *Environmental:* as the same economic function can be served with a reduction in the quantity of materials required in doing so.

In addition, Möslein and Kölling (2007) suggest that a hybrid value creation strategy bears the potential to create radically new offerings and solutions even for unknown problems and undefined demands. The aforementioned examples, such as the poshbags4rent, Kindle, Flexpetz and miCoach offerings, have in fact created new markets and defined previously unknown needs of customers. Another old and simple example to understand the potential of hybrid value creation is that of the pizza delivery service. Going back in time, the first pizza delivery service, a classic product–service combination, was radically innovative. Very often one does not seem to realize the extent of value innovation in this product–service offering. By delivering the pizza to customers' homes, the first delivery service broke the existing industry-specific procedure that people went to a restaurant to eat. It also created a whole new market. Today one cannot imagine a world without pizza delivery.

It is clear from the existing research literature and the previously mentioned examples that hybrid value creation is a phenomenon that is growing in importance. However, even though extant research has identified that hybrid value creation is a widespread phenomenon and explained the arguments underpinning its increasing popularity it has failed to systematically explain what really creates value in different business models of hybrid value creation. It is also obvious that dynamics of hybrid value creation in the different examples mentioned above vary considerably, even though they all strive to combine products and services. In other words, value creation as in the case of Rolls-Royce - by selling hot air - differs substantially from value creation as in the case of the miCoach offering or the PoshBags4rent rental service. Thus, the goal of this dissertation is to throw light on how value is created in different business models of hybrid value creation.

By reading this dissertation, the reader will learn the following. First, there are four unique clusters of hybrid value creation business models, namely *embedded products*, *leasing/renting/sharing/pooling*, *mass customization*, and *solutions*. Second, different value creating attributes - *individualization, marketing-integration, operational-integration,* and *firm–customer interaction* - are crucial for the success of these unique clusters. Third, design is critical for the success of embedded products. And fourth, strategic innovation is vital to be financially successful when providing solutions.

These conclusions were drawn from data collected not only from large industrial firms such as Electrolux, Siemens, and Viessmann, but also from arguably more innovative firms such as Adidas, Amazon, and Apple. This dissertation provides a systematic assessment of hybrid value creation and identifies empirically derived strategies for hybrid value creation. In addition, it helps practitioners to come to grips with the dynamics of hybrid value creation, irrespective of the industry they are in. At the same time directions for future research are identified and provided.

The remainder of this part is organized as follows. In chapter 2, a definition of hybrid value creation is systematically derived and illustrated in the context of the Rolls-Royce and the MyMuesli examples. Finally, chapter 3 provides a detailed overview of the structure of this dissertation.

# 2 Defining Hybrid Value Creation

As previously mentioned, this dissertation focuses on understanding the dynamics of value creation in different hybrid value creation business models. Before delving deeper into hybrid value creation, it is important to define the phenomenon. In order to do so, first, a definition of value creation is provided and then the denotation of the prefix "hybrid" is elucidated.

To define value creation, one needs first to understand two concepts of value which are *"use value"* and *"exchange value"* (Bowman and Ambrosini 2000). Use value refers to the specific qualities of the product perceived by customers in relation to their needs. Use value is a subjective and individualistic concept. Exchange value refers to price. It is the monetization realized at a single point in time when goods are exchanged. Exchange value is an accounting convenience. Combining these two concepts, Lepak, Smith, and Taylor (2007: 182) suggest that:

> *"... value creation depends on the relative amount of value that is subjectively realized by a target user (or buyer) who is the focus of value creation – whether individual, organization, or society – and that this subjective value realization must at least translate into the user's willingness to exchange a monetary amount for the value received".*

They state that for value creation to endure:

1. Exchange value (monetary amount) must exceed the producer's cost (this includes money, time, effort, joy, and the like); without which the producer is making a loss;
2. This exchange value depends on the perceived positive performance excess difference between the new use value proposed (from the new focal task, product, or service) and the closest existing alternatives (current task, product, or service) the customer has; without a positive performance difference perceived by the customer, it is value destruction.

They also further state that:

> *"In general, without these excesses, neither the user nor the creator of value would be willing to repeatedly engage in these activities over the long term"* (2007: 182).

The term "hybrid" denotes the presence of two separate kinds of components in an offering:

1. The presence of a product (i.e. tangible component);
2. The presence of a service (i.e. intangible component).

Hence, hybrid value creation is defined as the process of generating additional value by innovatively combining products (tangible component) and services (intangible component).

This definition of hybrid value creation is transferred to the Rolls-Royce and MyMuesli examples. In the case of Rolls-Royce, through its trademarked *'power-by-the-hour'* contracts, an innovative combination of products (engines and spare parts) and services (repairs and preventive maintenance), the firm has taken over complete responsibility for keeping the engines running. By doing so, its customers are given an exact cost projection to the last cent. This way, Rolls-Royce takes over the risk associated with engine breakdowns and creates value for its customers.

In the case of MyMuesli, by contrast, the firm creates value for its customers by providing a unique breakfast cereal to meet the exact tastes of each individual customer. Hence, customers are willing to pay a premium for the perceived positive performance excess the customized cereal brings to them, when they compare it to other alternatives available in the market. The service is integrated in the final product, as it is in the form of individualization that is conducted in preparing the cereal.

# 3 The Structure of the Thesis

This dissertation follows a research path that can be best described as a step-by-step process in order to achieve its goal, i.e., understanding the dynamics of value creation in different product–service combinations. It is structured into six parts. Each part is broken down into chapters. The chapters are further split into sections and subsections.

Part I is the introduction, which sets the stage for this dissertation. This is followed by parts II, III, IV, and V, which are modular in structure and consist of a systematic literature review and three empirical studies. These parts are largely self-contained in nature and focus on specific research questions. Hence they may be read independently. Part VI concludes this dissertation by providing a summary of contributions. In addition, based on the systematic literature review and the three empirical studies, implications for practice and directions for future research are provided. Below an overview of each of the six parts and how they build on each other is presented. *Figure 1* provides an overview of the dissertation.

*Part I – Introduction: Setting the Stage*

This part starts by elucidating the rationale and relevance of this dissertation topic. Then a definition for hybrid value creation is theoretically derived. Finally, an overview of the structure of this thesis is provided.

*Part II – Systematic Literature Review: Hybrid Value Creation*

A systematic literature review was essential because the substantial body of literature addressing different aspects of hybrid value creation is scattered and is split into many different strands. Consequently, this part provides a state-of-the-art report on hybrid value creation by first systematically identifying and then analyzing 169 publications in the field. In the process research from different strands is brought together, analyzed and classified into eight categories: (1) *the strategic view*; (2) *the organization view*; (3) *the marketing view*; (4) *the design view*; (5) *the innovation view*; (6) *the business level view*; (7) *sustainability aspects*; and (8) *the macroeconomic perspective*. Research in each of these categories is summarized and research gaps are identified. Based on their links and interactions, a map of the research field is suggested. This part also provides a discussion and reflects on the findings with respect to the pervasiveness of literature in the field and the research methods used. It concludes by identifying that there is a lack of understanding of how value is created in different product-service combinations. This is also established as a dominant strategic research gap in the overall research landscape.

**I. Introduction: Setting the stage**
- States the relevance of hybrid value creation
- Defines hybrid value creation
- Provides the structure of the thesis

**II. Systematic Literature Review: Hybrid Value Creation**
- Identifies, analyzes and consolidates 169 crucial publications into eight categories
- Suggests a research map based on links and interactions
- Identifies research gaps and directions for future research

**III. Empirical Study 1: The Four Clusters of Hybrid Value Creation**
- Identifies four value-creating attributes from literature
- Develops four distinct clusters of hybrid value creation
- Derives the role of the four value-creating attributes in each cluster
- Identifies the crucial value-creating attribute for each cluster
- Concludes by identifying two clusters – embedded products and solutions – that require further research

**IV. Empirical Study 2: The Cluster of Embedded Products**
- Explores the cluster of embedded products
- Identifies two groups of critical aspects that influence the design of embedded products

**V. Empirical Study 3: The Cluster of Solutions**
- Explores the cluster of solutions
- Identifies new service offerings
- Illustrates and explains solution-based business models using the value innovation framework

**VI. Discussion and Conclusion**
- Summary of research conducted
- Implications for practice
- Provides directions for future research

*Figure 1: Structure of the thesis*

*Part III – Empirical Study 1: The Four Clusters of Hybrid Value Creation*

This part focuses on understanding how and where value is created in different business models of hybrid value creation, which was identified as a dominant research gap in the systematic literature review. To close this gap, this study investigates 80 successful offerings of hybrid value creation and provides an organizational perspective to this challenge. To achieve this goal, first, four value-creating attributes – *individualization, marketing-integration, operational-integration,* and *firm–customer interaction* - are identified from literature. Second, using a deductive case analysis, four distinct clusters of hybrid value creation are developed. These are: *embedded products, leasing/renting/sharing/pooling, mass customization,* and *solutions.* Next, the role and impact of the four value creating attributes for each cluster is systematically derived. As a result, a two-step strategy for the successful design of hybrid offerings is suggested: when implementing hybrid value creation, first, the type of hybrid value creation has to be determined and then depending on the cluster the corresponding key value-creating attribute(s) need to be designed. The study concludes by identifying two clusters - *embedded products* and *solutions* - that require further research. This is necessary to gain a deeper understanding of the logic of value creation in these two clusters. In the following two parts, these are independently studied (embedded products is explored in part IV, solutions in part V). The other two clusters are identified to have grown into independent research subjects and hence are excluded from the focus of this dissertation.

*Part IV – Empirical Study 2: The Cluster of Embedded Products*

Building on the findings of part III (empirical study 1), this part further explores the cluster of embedded products. In part III, operational-integration is identified as the main value-creating attribute for embedded products. Hence, it becomes imperative that offerings from this cluster are immaculately designed. Consequently, this study focuses on the first step of the design process in the context of embedded products. This leads us to the research question: what are the critical aspects that need to be taken into consideration when designing an embedded product? To answer this, an explorative qualitative case study approach is used. Semi-structured interviews are conducted with product and marketing managers in six firms that offer embedded products. The six firms cover a broad range of embedded products: *an e-book reader, a fitness machine, a gaming console, a music player, a programmable toy,* and *a web-based personal trainer*. The analysis and iterative comparison of the interview data derives six critical aspects that influence the design of hybrid products. Three critical aspects - *hybrid arrangement, dimension of hybridity,* and *revenue model used* - are identified to be strategically oriented. The other three critical aspects - *web as a service platform, engagement in community building,* and *integration of customer feedback* - are identified to be service-oriented. This empirical study also sheds some light on how these critical aspects are related to each other. The findings help both firms and researchers that want to better understand and design embedded products. Overall, the findings show that firms do not really know how to integrate the service dimension to use it as a driver for value creation. Nevertheless, all firms exhibited the urge to improve their service dimension.

*Part V – Empirical Study 3: The Cluster of Solutions*

Building on the findings of part III (empirical study I), this part further explores the cluster of solutions. In part III, marketing-integration is identified as the main value-creating attribute for solutions. In line with this, manufacturing firms in the recent past are going downstream and providing complementary services to be more successful. However, research has identified that firms have not been financially successful with a move downstream into services. Even though this leads to an increase in overall sales (turnover) for firms, their profitability as a percentage of sales is actually decreasing. Hence this study, using a strategic innovation perspective, explains how firms can go about achieving profitability by providing marketing-integration. This leads us to the research question: what should be the logic behind a firm's strategy to implement a solution-based business model? To answer this, the study builds on existing theoretical contributions by drawing from exploratory case study research undertaken with four international firms operating in different industries: *laundry systems (Electrolux)*, *healthcare systems (Siemens)*, *climate control systems (Viessmann)*, and *cleaning systems (Wetrok)*. A cross case analysis identifies five distinct service offerings: *business consulting services*, *comprehensive services*, *educational services*, *financial services*, and *information management services*. In sum, the analysis reveals that to be successful in a solution-based business model firms need to aim for strategic innovation. They need to focus not only on increasing buyer value by meeting customer needs better, but also on reducing cost structures by eliminating resource wastefulness. To achieve these contradictory goals, firms need to exploit their tacit knowledge of their products and industry.

*Part VI – Discussion and Conclusions*

This part concludes this dissertation by providing a summary of contributions. In addition it provides a holistic view of the implications for practice and directions for future research based on the results of the four encompassing research studies.

# II

## Systematic Literature Review: Hybrid Value Creation

# 1 The Rise of Hybrid Value Creation

Hybrid value creation, i.e. the process of generating additional value by innovatively combining products (tangible components) and services (intangible components), is gaining popularity as services have become an omnipresent part of firms' strategic mission and corporate planning (Vandermerwe 2000). This chapter first looks at the arguments in favor of hybrid value creation in detail. Second it identifies the barriers and hurdles that inhibit the success and growth of hybrid value creation. Third, it explains why a systematic review of the field is an important contribution. Finally, the goals of this systematic literature review[1] and the approach used to achieve them are explained.

## 1.1 Arguments in Favor

The arguments underpinning the increasing popularity of such product-service offerings in today's business environment are manifold: product-service combinations offer higher returns due to shrinking margins for manufactured goods (Windahl and Lakemond 2006). Revenue streams from services are less likely to be adversely affected by downturns in the economy, when compared to revenue streams generated from the sale of capital goods (Brady, Davies, and Gann 2005a; 2005b). By offering such integrated solutions, firms move up the value chain and, hence, easily differentiate themselves from their competitors (Zaring et al. 2001). Hybrid value creation is an effective strategy for companies from advanced economies, where cost leadership is not an option, to face the force of globalization (Vandermerwe and Rada 1988). Hybrid value creation offerings are more difficult to imitate as the service aspect is less visible leading to sustainable competitive advantage (Heskett, Sasser, and Schlesinger 1997). There are environmental benefits of decoupling ownership of assets and use through the introduction of product-service combinations (Mont 2004a). Also, customers increasingly pay more attention to life cycle costs than before (Hartmann and Girmscheid 2004) and therefore demand complete solutions, i.e. the combination of products and services. Increased interaction between customers and suppliers leads to customized solutions, which

[1] Note that a refined version of this literature review has been published in the *Journal für Betriebswirtschaft* (see Velamuri, Neyer, and Möslein 2011). Although that publication was co-authored, the research strategy for identifying publications, the categorization of identified publications, the identification of research gaps, and the analysis of identified publications for additional insights are primarily attributable to Vivek K. Velamuri.

fit customers' needs better, which in turn pushes the demand for such solutions from customers (Davies 2004). For instance, Windahl et al. (2004) have illustrated how interaction between customer and supplier can lead to an integrated solution provided by the conglomerate Asea Brown Boveri's [ABB] Facility Management Division (FMD). The division's original core business can be broken down into two parts. The first is to install climate control systems produced and sold by another division of the conglomerate. The second is to provide after-sales service to the installed base. A longtime customer suggested that FMD should not only provide a climate control system but also take over the day-to-day operations of the system. Negotiations led to a contract, in which the FMD was given a percentage of the energy savings on the precondition that it also financed the investment.

As seen from this example, one of the core ideas of hybrid value creation is to build unique relationships with customers and enhance customer loyalty. This is achieved through an integrated combination of products and services, allowing for the meeting of customer needs better than a standalone product or service (Tukker 2004).

## 1.2 Barriers and Hurdles

Literature also points out barriers and hurdles that may limit the popularity and acceptance of product-service offerings. To begin with, existing culture itself could be an inherent obstacle for the acceptance of such business models (Manzini and Vezzoli 2002). They state that a culture shift is needed from two sides, i.e. first, the customers must be open to accept such offerings, and second the businesses require a change in the corporate culture and organization to design, develop, and deliver such offerings. Another major hurdle identified is that firms may not believe in the economic potential of product-service offerings (Oliva and Kallenberg 2003). This might also be magnified by aspects which, on first glance, may seem farfetched, but on close examination may actually play a significant role in diminishing the economic potential of product-service offerings. For instance, Zaring et al. (2001) mention that there is evidence that tax regimes currently used could disfavor product-service arrangements when compared to product sales. Beyond pure economic reasons, the lack of competencies required to offer such solutions was identified as another reason why firms may decide against product-service systems (Oliva and Kallenberg 2003). In other words, firms may not be in a position to align their organization, as required, to successfully offer integrated product-service combinations.

This is because firms need to do more than just overhaul their sales force to be successful (Bennett, Sharma, and Tipping 2001). Firms also need to develop and/or acquire new capabilities, as they must shift from being product- or service-centric to being customer-centric (Brady, Davies, and Gann 2005a). Similarly, firms may also need new metrics and incentives as the focus shifts from a single transaction to a relationship with the customer (Windahl et al. 2004). Overall, previous research underlines that an extended set of competencies is needed to provide hybrid solutions when compared to providing standalone products or services (Reichwald and Piller 2009; Shepherd and Ahmed 2000; Tukker 2004; Windahl et al. 2004).

## 1.3 Why the Review?

Given the increased importance of and interest in hybrid value creation, it has been the center of enquiry for many researchers from different parts of the world. Not surprisingly, these researchers have used different terms to describe the same phenomenon. This has led to various independent strands of research, albeit with different focuses, that can be amalgamated as research done on the phenomenon of hybrid value creation. It must be also noted that researchers from these different strands have often ignored research conducted by other strands. This review is required to paint an overall picture of the field.

## 1.4 Goals and Approach

The literature review has three goals:

1. To deliver a state-of-the-art report on hybrid value creation including a concise set of current definitions of key concepts and their origins
2. To suggest a first categorization of the field that is developed from the identified literature and the underlying key concepts
3. To identify research gaps and directions for potentially fruitful future research.

With these objectives in mind, this literature review first systematically identifies and then analyses 169 publications in the field of hybrid value creation. Second, it clusters the identified publications into eight categories. Based on these categories and their links and interactions, it suggests a mapping of the field. Finally, the review discusses and reflects the findings with respect to the pervasiveness of literature in the field, the research methods used, and the potential areas for further research.

# 2 Research Strategy and Analysis

This chapter first explains the research strategy used in identifying the publications dealing with the phenomenon of hybrid value creation. Then it provides an analysis of the publication and identifies different strands of research dealing with the same. It finally concludes with an overview of the most prolific authors for each strand/term. The overview also includes information on where these authors come from in terms of geography and discipline. The overall process comprising both the research strategy and analysis is summarized in *Figure 2*.

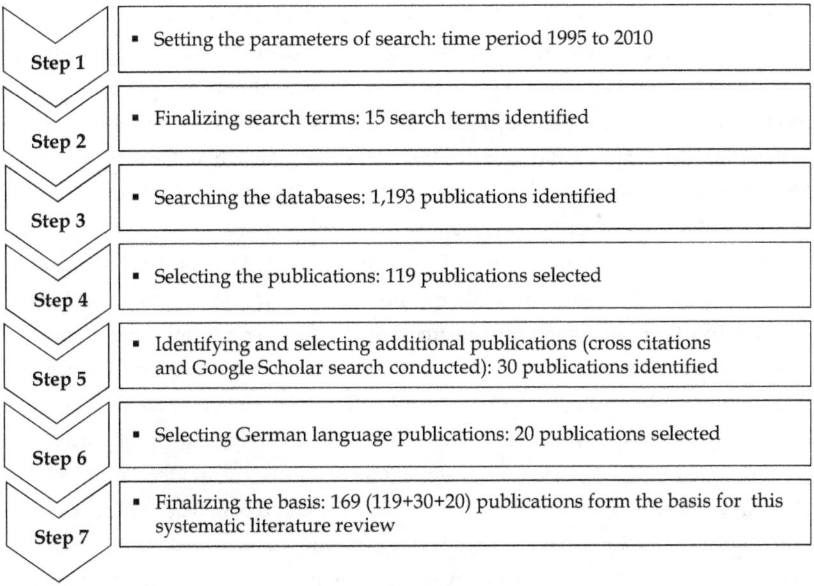


*Figure 2: Overview of research approach – systematic literature review*

## 2.1 Research Strategy

Systematic literature reviews in the social sciences are a relatively recent phenomenon. Unlike traditional narrative reviews, a systematic literature review has to follow a clear review protocol and to state explicitly its methods of selecting and evaluating publications in the field of interest (Tranfield, Denyer, and Smart

2003; Pittaway et al. 2004; Möslein 2005). The research strategy of the present review is therefore detailed in the following.

First, the parameters are set, defining the depth and scope of the search strategy. As hybrid value creation is a relatively new concept, despite some early developments in the 1980s, the focus of this review is - in a first step - set on literature published in or after 1995 till the end of 2010. To ensure high quality of publications, the first search step only takes into account international peer-reviewed journal publications. Follow-up search steps also capture relevant knowledge from earlier sources (as far as quoted in the first set) and other sources (like publications in industrialist outlets) to complement the set of findings.

Next, the search terms are defined. The following key terms associated with hybrid value creation are identified (listed in alphabetical order): complex product system, customer solutions, dematerialization, extended products, functional products, functional economy, hybrid product, hybrid solution, integrated solution, product based service, product related service, product service, product service system, productization, and servitization. Premier research databases including EBSCO Business Source Complete, SCOPUS, and WISO are searched using the above-mentioned keywords. The resulting set of publications is complemented with selected publications in the German language dealing with hybrid value creation. The rationale for this inclusion of German publications is twofold: first, hybrid value creation has been an important research area in the German-speaking countries, especially in Germany, in the past few years. The German Federal Ministry for Education and Research (in German, BMBF - Bundesministerium für Bildung und Forschung) identified hybrid value creation as one of the key growth opportunities for the famed small and medium-scale enterprises in Germany, the engine of the German economy. In line with that, over 100 full-time researchers split in 15 fully funded BMBF projects have researched on hybrid value creation. Second, this publication originates from a German research institution and the authors are convinced that literature reviews are a valuable mechanism to make research accessible in a systematic way, even across the boundaries of languages or publication formats. Hence, research[2] done in Germany and published in the German language is also included in this review.

[2] In line with German academic culture, dissertations have also been included.

## 2.2 Analysis

Initially, the results of the database search identified in total 1,193 publications in the English language in or after 1995 (excluding book reviews and editorials) for further examination. After an initial screening of the identified publications, 119 were shortlisted as directly relevant to the research enquiry. The list, along with the initial search results and the number of shortlisted publications for each search term or string of terms, is reported in *Table 1*.

*Table 1: Initial search results and the number of shortlisted publications*

| SNo. | Search Term | Total number of publications | Shortlisted publications |
|---|---|---|---|
| 1 | complex product system | 87 | 13 |
| 2 | customer solution | 43 | 11 |
| 3 | dematerialization | 61 | 2 |
| 4 | extended product | 134 | 4 |
| 5 | functional economy | 181 | 1 |
| 6 | functional product | 11 | 3 |
| 7 | hybrid product | 123 | 2 |
| 8 | hybrid solution | 76 | 0 |
| 9 | integrated solution | 164 | 17 |
| 10 | product based service | 7 | 0 |
| 11 | product related service | 43 | 9 |
| 12 | product service system | 119 | 39 |
| 13 | productization | 34 | 1 |
| 14 | servitization | 29 | 9 |
| 15 | product service* | 81 | 8 |
| **Total** | | **1,193** | **119** |

* Limited to a title search

In addition, crucial citations referenced within these 119 publications were included to capture publications (though again conference proceedings were excluded) preceding 1995. An internet search conducted using Google Scholar identified further publications from the industry side which are out of the scope of academic databases, but can still be classified as relevant for the advancement of work on hybrid value creation. In order to capture this body of knowledge, publications from quarterlies and internal publications of consultancy firms were also taken into consideration. In total 30 new publications were added to our review. Furthermore,

20 German-language publications identified as most relevant with the help of two experts[3] in the field of hybrid value creation are also added. These 20 publications have been chosen from a list of publications on hybrid value creation provided by the Projektträger im Deutschen Zentrum für Luft- und Raumfahrt (PT-DLR, Project Management Agency - part of the German Aerospace Center). In the end, 169 (119+30+20) publications formed the basis of this literature review.

## 2.3 Various Research Strands

Overall, the strategic importance of combining products and services has led to an increase of literature dealing with the phenomenon of combining products and services. The literature review revealed many definitions dealing with this concept. The first definition found chronologically for each term has been listed in *Table 2*.

Analyzing the publications, it emerged that "*product service systems*" (PSS), with over 30 academic publications, is a distinct strand of research dealing with combining products and services. The focus of this strand is predominantly on reducing the negative environment impact by combining products and services. This is also evident by the fact that 16 publications identified are published in the *Journal for Cleaner Production*. The first to publish using the term PSS were Goedkoop et al. (1999). However, the most prolific author is Oksana Mont, who clarified the concept of PSS and identified the four main elements of a PSS as product, service, actor networks, and infrastructure. She contributed immensely to understanding the viability of sharing and second-life business models. Most publications from this strand have originated from Europe, mostly from the UK and Sweden. The contributing authors prior to 2009 were from the disciplines of environment, sustainability, and economics. But for most publications in 2009, authors came from engineering and design disciplines.

[3] The experts have more than four years of research experience in the field of hybrid value creation.

*Table 2: Different concepts dealing with the same phenomenon*

| Term | First definition# found chronologically for each term | Citation |
|---|---|---|
| **Complex Product Systems** | "Complex product systems (CoPS) can be defined as high cost, engineering and information technology intensive, customised products having **large numbers of tailored subsystems and components.**" | Hansen and Rush 1998: 555 |
| **Customer Solutions** | "In all sorts of industries, companies that traditionally have made and sold stand-alone products are changing their strategies. They are creating high value solutions **by integrating various products and services** - even merging supplier's and customer's operations - to solve a complete customer problem." | Foote et al. 2001: 84 |
| **Demateria-lization** | "Dematerialization, indicates a focus on functions and needs, and a significant departure from today's practices." | Dobers and Wolff 1999: 31 |
| **Full Service** | "... comprehensive **bundles of products and/or services**, that fully satisfy the needs and wants of a customer related to a specific event or problem." | Stremersch, Wuyts, and Frambach 2001: 1 |
| **Functional Products** | "Functional products, also known as 'total care products', are products that comprise **combinations of 'hard' and 'soft' elements.**" | Alonso-Rasgado et al. 2004: 515 |
| **Integrated Solutions** | "A third effective business model is to **combine products and services** into a seamless offering that addresses a pressing customer need." | Wise and Baumgartner 1999: 138 |
| **Product Service Systems** | "A Product Service system (PS system) is a **marketable set of products and services** capable of jointly fulfilling a user's need." | Goedkoop et al. 1999*: 18 |
| **Product-Related Services** | "... essential component in an **integrated package** of products designed to meet all the requirements of demanding customers." | Stille 2003: 195 |
| **Serviti-zation** | "Modern corporations are offering fuller market packages or 'bundles' of customer-focussed **combinations of goods, services, support, self-service, and knowledge.** But services are beginning to dominate." | Vandermerwe and Rada 1988: 314 |

# Emphasis added

* This definition is not from an academic journal but from a report entitled *"Product Service-Systems – Ecological and Economic Basics"*, commissioned by the Dutch Ministries of Environment and Economic Affairs. Subsequently it has been cited by the majority of authors.

*Complex product systems* (*CoPS*) and *integrated solutions,* with 13 and 17 academic publications respectively, also stake claim to being independent strands of research. *CoPS* tend to be one-off projects, where the service element is limited to design, project management, system engineering, and systems integration (Hobday and Rush 1999). An example of *CoPS* is the production of an aircraft engine with a detailed specification to meet the exact requirements of a demanding customer. Here the engine is the product, whereas the service aspect is the design, project management, and system integration required to produce the engines and the after-sales service provided to the customer. Recent evidence shows that providers of *CoPS* strive to extend their revenue streams by delivering service-intensive offerings and meeting the final need of the customer (Hobday, Davies, and Prencipe 2005). For example, Rolls-Royce, the world's second-largest maker of large jet engines, has successfully extended its revenue stream by meeting the final need of the customer through service-intensive offerings.

This goal is consistent with that of an *integrated solutions* strategy (Davies 2004). Hence, *integrated solutions* are an extension of *CoPS* and together they form a research strand that focuses on product service combinations for complex offerings. Also it is important to note that *integrated solutions* and *CoPS* have a group of researchers in common, who are based in the UK, affiliated to "The CoPS Innovation Centre", a joint venture between SPRU - Science and Technology Policy Research at the University of Sussex and the CENTRIM - Centre for Research in Innovation Management at the University of Brighton. Most researchers from this group come from management (specializing in innovation) and engineering disciplines and the most prolific authors are Andrew Davies, Michael Hobday and Tim Brady. These researchers have mainly contributed in two domains: i) understanding the innovation dynamics in CoPS; and ii) clarifying the role of system integrators for delivering integrated solutions.

The rest of the concepts do not have a substantial number of publications and/or lack a clear enough focus to be considered as a stream of research. "*Dematerialization*" focuses on absolute or relative reduction in the quantity of materials required to serve economic functions. Authors argue that if business models are appropriately adapted and customers do not see single ownership of products as a personal requisite, then it can lead to a reduction in the detrimental environmental effects (Meijkamp 1998). For example, business models involving car-sharing is a popular example of a community serving its standard of economic functions albeit through a reduction in the materials used. Another example, similar to the aforementioned Rolls-Royce selling power by the hour, is the massive change in the copying machine business models. Instead of first selling copying machines and then charging for office supplies and repair separately, firms are now focusing on charging their customers a fixed price per copy and are taking over total responsibility for the availability of the machine. Such a business model on the one hand encourages the customers to minimize the number of printouts, as they pay separately for each copy the machine churns out. On the other hand, it also interests the firm to produce sturdier machines and focus on reducing input wastage. As seen from the above-mentioned examples, dematerialization is a goal that should be achieved through the introduction of PSS. Authors using the term *dematerialization* are primarily based in Scandinavia.

Even though Levitt was the first to hint towards the solution business when he introduced the "total product concept" (Levitt 1980), Vandermerwe and Rada (1988) were the first to delve deeper into the concept when they introduced the concept of *servitization* as an approach to change the competitive dynamics of a firm. By going downstream and providing complementary services, firms can not only generate additional revenues, but they can also differentiate themselves from their competitors. This can be seen as a strategy for manufacturing firms in the advanced economies to compete on terms other than just costs. The authors listed six arguments for servitization as a competitive tool. These are: i) setting up barriers to competitors; ii) setting up barriers to third parties; iii) setting up barriers to customers; iv) making customers dependent; v) differentiating the market offering; and vi) diffusing new innovation.

The remaining terms, "*customer solutions*", "*functional products*" (also known as total care products), "*product related services*", and "*full service*" are also used to describe product-service offerings. The preference to use a specific term by researchers can be attributed to the fact that they come from different geographies or different disciplines. *Customer solution* is widely used in the strategy and marketing literature to describe product-service offerings that solve specific customer problems. Literature on *customer solution* is narrative, with anecdotal examples and no concrete research data. The term *functional product* is solely used in the UK. Whereas the term *product related services* is popular in the German language area. *Full service* has been used in the marketing discipline.

An overview of who the most prolific author is (based on different search terms), where they come from in terms of geography and discipline, and in which journals they publish, can be found for selected search terms in *Table 3*.

*Table 3: Who has published? Where from? And in which journal?*

| Term (number of papers) | Most prolific geography (number of papers)* | Other geographies (Number of papers)* | Most prolific author(s) (Number of papers) | Most prolific journal (s) (Number of papers) | Most contributions from which discipline |
|---|---|---|---|---|---|
| Complex Product Systems (13) | UK (13) | Canada, Italy, Sweden (1) | Hobday, M. (5); Davies, A. (4) | Industrial and Corporate Change (4); Research Policy (3) | Innovation Management, Engineering |
| Customer Solutions (11) | USA (10) | Canada, France, Singapore, Switzerland, UK (1) | Galbraith, J. (3) | Marketing Management, Booz Allen and Hamilton internal publication, McKinsey Quarterly (2) | Marketing, Strategy, Organizational Studies |
| Dematerialization (2) | Denmark, Sweden (1) | | Jespersen, J., Dobers, P. (1) | Business Strategy and the Environment, European Environment (1) | Economics, Environment |
| Full Service (2) | NL (2) | US (1) | Stremersch, S. (2) | Journal of Marketing, Industrial Marketing Management (1) | Marketing |
| Functional Products (3) | UK (3) | Sweden (1) | Alonso-Rasgado, T., Thompson, G. (2) | Journal of Engineering Design (2) | Engineering, Industrial Design |
| Integrated Solutions (17) | UK (9) | Sweden (2); Canada, Italy, USA (1) | Davies, A. (5); Brady, T. (4) | Industrial Marketing Management (2) | Engineering, Operations |
| Product Service Systems (39) | UK (11); Sweden(10) | Denmark (5); Germany (4); Austria, Finland, Netherlands, Italy, Japan (2) | Mont, O. (6); Morelli, N.(4); Roy, R. (3) | Journal of Cleaner Production (16) Journal of Manufacturing Technology Management (6) | Environment, Sustainability, Design, Engineering |
| Product-Related Services (9) | Switzerland (3) | Germany (2); UK, Finland, USA, France (1) | Gebauer, H. (3) Fleisch, E., Krempl, R. (2) | Economic Bulletin (2) | Industrial Services |
| Servitization (9) | UK (8) | Switzerland (1) | Vandermerwe, S. (2) | Journal of Manufacturing Technology Management (3) | Marketing, Operations |

* Some papers have been counted more than once as they have been authored by people coming from more than one country.

# 3 Research Categories

This chapter deals with the categorization of the identified publications. First, the approach used to categorize the 169 publications into eight broad categories is described. Second, research done in each of the eight categories - defined in the previous step - is summarized.

The final selection consisting of 169 publications was first completely read and categorized based on a full-text analysis. Each publication was tagged with 3-4 keywords such as competitive advantage, pricing, sustainability, organizational design, organization capabilities, business models, system integration, etc. Then the publications were clustered into 20 sub-groups based on the keyword tags given to them. The largest sub-group consists of 15 publications and the smallest of 3 publications. To provide better navigation through the 20 sub-groups and the publications itself, these sub-groups are clustered into eight logical broader categories. Formal content coding was not applied for this categorization. Hence, these categories should only be taken as an organizing tool, to get a clear overview of published research in this field, and not as a definitive categorization of the body of research.

*Table 4: Research categories*

| Areas | Topics included | No. of publications |
|---|---|---|
| Strategic view | Competitive advantage; concepts and barriers | 21 |
| Organization view | Organizational design; networks; organizational capabilities; system integration | 33 |
| Marketing view | Pricing; customer satisfaction | 23 |
| Design view | Strategic perspective; design process; design attributes | 16 |
| Innovation view | Innovation management; firms in and processes for transition | 24 |
| Business level view | Business models; viability in specific industries; engineering and information technology | 29 |
| Sustainability aspects | Human behavior and consumption; evaluation of sustainability | 11 |
| Macroeconomic perspective | Prevalence and effect; policy making | 12 |
| **Total number of publications** | | **169** |

*Table 4* lists the different categories with the topics included and the number of publications for each category. A graphical representation of the categories can be found in *Figure 3*.

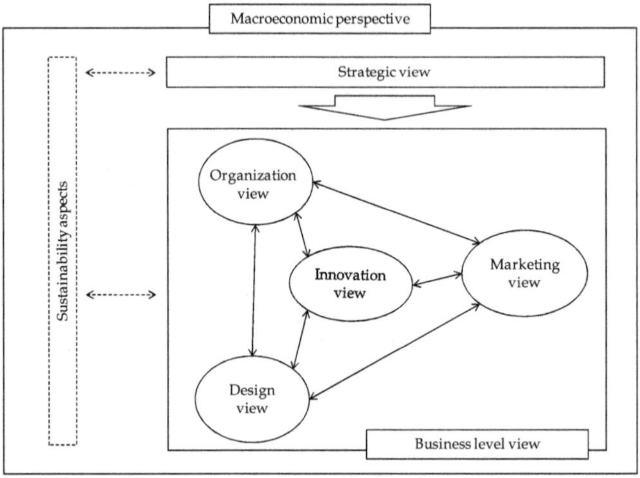


*Figure 3: Overview of categories*

Below research from each of the eight categories is summed up in a systematic manner. First, each category is briefly explained and the sub-groups contained are listed. Then research from each sub-group is presented and summarized.

## 3.1 The Strategic View

The strategic view contains publications that primarily focus on why it makes sense to combine products and services and what the drivers and barriers are for providing such combined offerings. These publications have been split into two sub-groups: '*competitive advantage*' and '*concepts and barriers*' (see *Table 5*).

*Competitive advantage* captures publications that revolve around changing the competitive dynamics a firm is in through joint product–service offerings. In the analyzed publications, there is an agreement that combining products and services can indeed improve the competitive bearing of a firm (e.g. Vandermerwe and Rada 1988). Although authors agree that the ultimate goal is to meet "customer needs" better in order to achieve competitive advantage, there is no consensus on how to do that. There is a suggestion that firms can use hybrid value creation as a differentiation strategy in mature industries (e.g. Robinson, Clarke-Hill, and Clarkson 2002). Authors have also suggested that hybrid value creation is an innovation strategy to find answers for currently undefined problems (e.g. Möslein and Kölling 2007).

*Concepts and barriers* contains publications that theoretically explain why firms should exploit the life cycle of products (e.g. Potts 1988). In addition they clarify the concept of integrated offerings (e.g. Mont 2002a; Buriánek et al. 2007; Nordin and Kowalkowski 2010) and divulge possible drivers for and barriers against combining products and services (e.g. Martin and Horne 1992). Research has also looked at result-based offerings, where managing mutual expectations between the supplier and customer has been identified as the key success factor (e.g. Ng and Nudurupati 2010). In sum, these publications help firms understand the phenomenon of hybrid value creation.

*Table 5: Research on the strategic view*

| Sub-topic | Study focus | Study | Year | Type |
|---|---|---|---|---|
| **Competitive advantage** | Servitization to change competitive dynamics | Vandermerwe and Rada | 1988 | Theoretical |
| | Why to bring in service perspective into factory operations | Chase and Erikson | 1992 | Narrative |
| | Importance of pre- and post-sale services for competitive advantage | Samli, Jacobs, and Wills | 1992 | Theoretical |
| | The economic rationale of after-sales service | Knecht, Leszinski, and Weber | 1993 | Narrative |
| | Why firms should focus on customer needs and not products | Phillips, Ochs, and Schrock | 1999 | Narrative |
| | Servitization to increase value creation and delivery to customers | Vandermerwe | 2000 | Case study |
| | Reasons for a move towards solutions | Brown | 2000 | Narrative |
| | Differentiation through service to gain competitive advantage | Robinson, Clarke-Hill, and Clarkson | 2002 | Case study |
| | Hybrid value creation as an innovation strategy | Möslein and Kölling | 2007 | Case study |
| | When is it advantageous to combine manufacturing and services: an historical perspective | Schmenner | 2010 | Theoretical |

| | | | | |
|---|---|---|---|---|
| **Concepts &barriers** | Exploiting life cycle of products | Potts | 1988 | Narrative |
| | Hurdles faced by manufacturing firms when changing focus towards services | Martin and Horne | 1992 | Exploratory interviews |
| | Clarifying product service systems | Mont | 2002a | Theoretical |
| | Drivers for and barriers against product service systems | Mont | 2002b | Case study |
| | Challenges and remedies for going downstream: demand and supply management | Auramo and Ala-Risku | 2005 | Case study |
| | Why manufacturing firms should focus on services | Araujo and Spring | 2006 | Theoretical |
| | Understanding the drivers of complexity in hybrid offerings | Buriánek et al. | 2007 | Theoretical |
| | What generates value in hybrid offerings | Schmitz | 2008 | Theoretical |
| | The concept of performance-based contracting in the manufacturing industry | Hypko, Tilebein, and Gleich | 2010a | Theoretical |
| | Risks and challenges associated with implementing outcome-based contracts | Ng and Nudurupati | 2010 | Case study |
| | Clarifying the concept of solutions | Nordin and Kowalkowski | 2010 | Conceptual |

## 3.2 The Organizational View

The organizational view compromises publications that focus on the inner view of the firm. It contains publications relating to organizational structure, competencies required, and positions on the value chain which firms strive to reach. The publications have been split into four sub-groups: '*organizational design*',' *networks*', '*organizational capabilities*', and '*system integration*' (see *Table 6*).

*Organizational design* contains publications that focus on the creation of roles, processes and formal relationships within an organization. They also contain publications on how to be customer centric (e.g. Galbraith 2002), design supply chains in the product-service context (e.g. Cohen, Agrawal, and Agrawal 2006; Johnson and Mena 2008), and align organizations to business models (e.g. Bennett, Sharma, and Tipping 2001). Authors agree that traditional organizational structures need to be modified to fit the demands and rigors of hybrid value creation.

*Networks* contains publications that identify that inter- and intra-firm relationship play a critical role for the development of integrated solutions (e.g. Windahl and Lakemond 2006) and provide insights to facilitate communication among various network partners (e.g. Denkena et al. 2009).

*Organizational capabilities* contains publications which focus on identifying capabilities required for providing product–service offerings (e.g. Shepherd and Ahmed 2000). For example, this includes capabilities required to become customer centric (e.g. Brady, Davies, and Gann 2005a; Bonnemeier, Buriánek, and Reichwald 2009), capabilities required to move up the value chain (e.g. Davies 2004), and capabilities required to improve the absorptive capacity of the firm (e.g. Davies and Brady 2000; Fischer et al. 2010). These publications are very closely connected to the organizational design publications and likewise there is a consensus among the authors that firms need a distinct set of capabilities for hybrid value creation. They have identified system integration, customer partnering, market knowledge and technical knowhow as the most critical capabilities.

*System integration* encompasses publications that focus on system integration as a core capability for a firm. Authors have contributed in explaining the value stream approach in high-technology capital goods (e.g. Hobday, Davies, and Prencipe 2005), why system integration plays a crucial role in capturing value, and how companies should go about it (Davies, Brady, and Hobday 2007).

*Table 6: Research on the organization view*

| Sub-topic | Study focus | Study | Year | Type |
|---|---|---|---|---|
| **Organizational design** | Two configurations of customer service orientations in manufacturing industry | Bowen, Siehl, and Schneider | 1989 | Theoretical |
| | Building strategically aligned business models | Bennett, Sharma, and Tipping | 2001 | Theoretical |
| | Organizational model for delivering solutions | Foote et al. | 2001 | Case study |
| | Organizing to be customer centric | Galbraith | 2002 | Case study |
| | Balancing capabilities and clients | Miller et al. | 2002 | Case study |
| | Supplier's view: a toolkit to design service operation | Johansson and Olhager | 2004 | Case study |
| | Success factors identified relating to internal behavioral dimension | Gebauer and Friedli | 2005 | Case study |
| | Toolkit for organizing spare-part and after-sales services | Cohen, Agrawal, and Agrawal | 2006 | Theoretical |
| | Changes required in a firm's activities, structure and culture | Gebauer, Friedli, and Fleisch | 2006 | Case study |
| | Environmental context, organizational structure and competencies | Ceci and Prencipe | 2008 | Case study |
| | Supply chain management | Johnson and Mena | 2008 | Case study |
| | Designing organizations in manufacturing | Neu | 2008 | Case study |

| | | | | |
|---|---|---|---|---|
| | firms to support complex service offerings | and Brown | | |
| | The need for new processes to avoid ignorance of potential risks | Molloy, Siemieniuch, and Sinclair | 2009 | Case study |
| | Finding the right organizational design for different services strategies | Gebauer et al. | 2010 | Quantitative |
| **Networks** | Importance of relationship within networks | Windahl and Lakemond | 2006 | Case study |
| | Approach to facilitate conversations among network partners | Krucken and Meroni | 2006 | Case study |
| | Importance of network of partners in plant engineering and construction | Schenk et al. | 2006 | Theoretical |
| | A model to facilitate cooperation between manufactures, software suppliers and consultants | Denkena et al. | 2009 | Theoretical |
| **Organizational capabilities** | Capability building model and organizational learning cycle | Davies and Brady | 2000 | Case study |
| | Competencies and organizational adjustments required | Shepherd and Ahmed | 2000 | Case study |
| | Creating a service firm in context of a manufacturing firm | Oliva and Kallenberg | 2003 | Case study |
| | Model for building project capabilities | Brady and Davies | 2004 | Case study |
| | Capabilities to move up the value stream | Davies | 2004 | Case study |
| | Extended set of competencies required | Windahl et al. | 2004 | Case study |
| | Factors that facilitate the formation of b2b services in goods-dominant firms | Neu and Brown | 2005 | Case study |
| | New skills required to be customer centric | Brady, Davies, and Gann | 2005a | Case study |
| | Organizing for repeatable solutions | Davies et al. | 2006 | Case study |
| | Ability to integrate customers – a crucial capability | Bonnemeier, Buriánek, and Reichwald | 2009 | Exploratory interviews |
| | Knowledge and information management – a crucial competency for efficient PSS | Goh and McMahon | 2009 | Theoretical |
| | Dynamic capabilities for developing services | Fischer et al. | 2010 | Case study |
| **System integration** | System integration: a core capability | Hobday, Davies, and Prencipe | 2005 | Case study |
| | System integrators in the aeronautical industry | Acha, Brusoni, and Prencipe | 2007 | Quantitative |
| | System seller vs. systems integrator | Davies, Brady, and Hobday | 2007 | Case study |

## 3.3 The Marketing View

Marketing, as defined by the American Marketing Association, is the activity, set of institutions, and processes for creating, communicating, delivering, and exchanging offerings that have value for customers, clients, partners, and society at large. In this paper, the marketing view has been limited to two sub-groups: *'pricing'* and *'customer satisfaction'* (see *Table 7*).

*Pricing* contains publications that not only focus on how to go about pricing, but also on communicating a price premium to the customer (e.g. Dostner and Roegner 2000; Roegner, Seifert, and Swinford 2001). It also contains publications that deal with estimating the value of combined offerings (e.g. Anderson and Narus 1995; Schuh et al. 2008; Grönroos and Helle 2010). The financial viability of some revenue models and strategies to compete on the basis of price are covered here (e.g. Docters et al. 2006). Also included are publications that focus on designing revenue models and the role of contracts as a control tool and coordination mechanism in the context of hybrid value creation (e.g. Buriánek et al. 2008; Buriánek 2009). Most authors agree that pricing is a twofold challenge that needs delicate handling. The first challenge is to calculate the appropriate premium and the second challenge is to communicate this premium to customers (in other words to justify the price premium to customers). The quandary lies in the fact that customers usually expect a discount as they see themselves as a 'Good Samaritan', who is doing a favor to their supplier by giving them a bigger chunk of the pie (e.g. Johansson, Krishnamurthy, and Schlissberg 2003).

*Customer satisfaction,* closely connected to the pricing sub-group, contains publications that focus on understanding customer satisfaction in the context of hybrid value creation (e.g. Klaus and Maklan 2007). In addition, publications that explain factors that influence customer acceptance of combined offerings are included (e.g. Maloney 2002; Rexfelt and Hirot af Ornas 2009). Authors agree that close customer interaction and a trust-based relationship are crucial success factors for not only improving customer satisfaction, but also for communicating the price premium to customers (Sharma, Iyer, and Evanschitzky 2008).

*Table 7: Research on the marketing view*

| Sub-topic | Study focus | Study | Year | Type |
|---|---|---|---|---|
| Pricing | Estimating the value of supplementary services | Anderson and Narus | 1995 | Case study |
| | Financial viability of the sharing business models | Prettenthaler and Steininger | 1999 | Quantitative |
| | Customer perspective to quantify a price premium | Doster and Roegner | 2000 | Case study |
| | Calculating and communicating the price of solutions | Roegner, Seifert, and Swinford | 2001 | Case study |
| | Criteria to evaluate full service contracts | Stremersch, Wuyts, and Frambach | 2001 | Case study |
| | Different kinds of bundles and their legality; classifies different bundling strategies | Stremersch and Tellis | 2002 | Theoretical |
| | The difference between solutions and bundles | Johansson, Krishnamurthy, and Schlissberg | 2003 | Case study |
| | Strategies to compete with bundling; replying to competitors bundling strategies | Docters et al. | 2006 | Case study |
| | Making services profitable in the context of small and medium sized enterprises | Malleret | 2006 | Case study |
| | A model to quantify customer value to help define prices of PSS | Ahlert et al. | 2008 | Theoretical |
| | Designing revenue models for hybrid offerings | Buriánek et al. | 2008 | Theoretical |
| | Price setting for hybrid offerings in machinery and engineering industry | Schuh et al. | 2008 | Theoretical |
| | Success factors in the price management of hybrid solutions | Bonnemeier | 2009 | Mixed methods |
| | Role of contracts as a control tool and coordination mechanism for PSS | Buriánek | 2009 | Case study |
| | A framework for measuring mutually created value between suppliers and customers in the manufacturing industry | Grönroos and Helle | 2010 | Conceptual |

| | | | | |
|---|---|---|---|---|
| **Customer satisfaction** | Improving customer satisfaction: aligning supply chain strategy to customer needs | Cohen et al. | 2000 | Case study |
| | Service encounters, perceived service quality and customer satisfaction | Maloney | 2002 | Theoretical |
| | Model to measure customer satisfaction in the context of service-based marketing | Klaus and Maklan | 2007 | Theoretical |
| | Diverging perceptions of suppliers and customers on solutions | Tuli, Kohli, and Bharadwaj | 2007 | Exploratory interviews |
| | Personal selling for increasing customer satisfaction in high-technology products | Sharma, Iyer, and Evanschitzky | 2008 | Theoretical |
| | Presents nine customer preference drivers relevant for PSS | Rese, Strotmann, and Karger | 2009 | Theoretical |
| | Two most important factors that influence customer acceptance of PSS within b2c context | Rexfelt and Hiort af Ornas | 2009 | Exploratory interviews |
| | Several propositions regarding customer preference for performance-based contracts in manufacturing industries | Hypko, Tilebein, and Gleich | 2010b | Conceptual |

## 3.4 The Design View

In this category, all publications that focus directly on and deal with all aspects pertaining to the design of product–service combinations have been included. These publications have been split into three sub-groups: *'strategic perspective'*, *'design processes'*, and *'design attributes'* (see *Table 8*).

*Strategic perspective* contains publications that focus on the importance of design (e.g. Manzini and Vezzoli 2002), the key strategic role design plays and the importance of taking multiple stakeholders input while designing (e.g. Evans, Partidário, and Lambert 2007). Authors agree that design plays a crucial role for the success of hybrid value creation. They conclude that design for hybrid value creation is different from that for traditional offerings as it requires the involvement of more stakeholders.

*Design process* contains publications that center on design process for services in the context of total care products, i.e. products where the supplier takes complete responsibility for the product and promises a certain function or performance to the customer (e.g. Alonso-Rasgado, Thompson, and Elfström 2004). There are also publications that emphasize a sustainable product and service development (SPSD) approach (e.g. Maxwell and van der Vorst 2003; Maxwell, Sheate, and van der Vorst 2006), as well as a life cycle oriented approach for designing PSS (e.g. Aurich, Fuchs, and Wagenknecht 2009). Although there has been research on the design process, it is very limited. To get a deeper theoretical understanding on the topic of design process in the context of hybrid value creation the publications listed are definitely not sufficient. Nevertheless, they provide a good starting point to study this topic.

*Design attributes* contains publications that focus on tools to identify actors involved (e.g. Morelli 2003), define requirements and measure final offerings (e.g. Moultrie, Clarkson, and Probert 2006). Additionally, there are publications that focus solely on systematically integrating customers in the design process (e.g. Morelli 2009). Also here, the literature is restricted but there is an agreement in the analyzed publications that a perspective shift is required and critical for identifying various parameters when designing for hybrid value creation.

*Table 8: Research on the design view*

| Sub-topic | Study focus | Study | Year | Type |
|---|---|---|---|---|
| **Strategic perspective** | Importance of design for successful PSS | Morelli | 2002 | Theoretical |
| | Need for a strategic perspective | Manzini and Vezzoli | 2002 | Case study |
| | Importance of input from multiple stakeholders for PSS design | Evans, Partidário, and Lambert | 2007 | Case study |
| **Design processes** | Developing sustainable products and services - a life cycle approach | Maxwell and van der Vorst | 2003 | Theoretical |
| | Services design in context of total care products | Alonso-Rasgado, Thompson, and Elfström | 2004 | Theoretical |
| | Life cycle oriented design of technical services | Aurich, Fuchs, and Wagenknecht | 2006 | Theoretical |
| | Rapid design process for total care products | Alonso-Rasgado and Thompson | 2006 | Theoretical |
| | Sustainable product service development approach to develop PSS | Maxwell, Sheate, and van der Vorst | 2006 | Case study |
| | Final phase of the design process of an product-related service | Lenfle and Midler | 2009 | Case study |
| | Method to systematically configure PSS offerings using a life cycle approach | Aurich et al. | 2009 | Theoretical |
| | How can products be adapted for PSS; Swedish design experiences | Sundin, Lindahl, and Ijomah | 2009 | Case study |

| | | | | |
|---|---|---|---|---|
| **Design attributes** | Perspective shift required to design PSS | Morelli | 2003 | Case study |
| | Product audit tool to measure all aspects of an offering | Moultrie, Clarkson, and Probert | 2006 | Theoretical |
| | Mapping actors involved and defining requirements | Morelli | 2006 | Theoretical |
| | Method to estimate customer satisfaction for conceptual design of PSS | Kimita, Shimomura, and Arai | 2009 | Theoretical |
| | Towards active participation of customers in the design of PSS | Morelli | 2009 | Theoretical |

## 3.5 The Innovation View

The innovation view contains publications that not only focus on innovation, but also deal with firms in transition from offering a standalone product or service to offering a product–service combination. The publications have been split into two sub-groups. They are *'innovation management'* and *'firms in and processes for transition'* (see *Table 9*).

*Innovation management* contains publications that deal with innovation management and dynamics of innovation in complex products (e.g. Miller et al. 1995), service-enhanced firms and product-related services (e.g. Gann and Salter 2000). Technology management and innovation process have also been discussed (e.g. Hobday and Rush 1998; Magnusson, Tell, and Watson 2005). Finally, there are publications that look at developing integrated solutions from customer- (e.g. Brax and Jonsson 2009) and serviced-centered perspectives (e.g. Windahl and Lakemond 2010). Authors agree and emphasize that innovation management in hybrid value creation differs from that in traditional value creation and therefore requires special procedures and practices to be successful. They suggest that firms need to understand how their customers use their products. For this they need to study the customer more deeply and grasp his value creating processes.

*Firms in and processes for transition* contains publications that focus on challenges faced by firms in transition and how incumbents react when faced with competition from new players offering product–service combinations (e.g. Hardstone 2004). Research has also looked at formulating service strategies for manufacturing firms (e.g. Frambach, Wels-Lips, and Gündlach 1997; Mathieu 2001; Homburg, Faßnacht, and Günther 2002; Gebauer, Bravo-Sanchez, and Fleisch 2008, Baines et al. 2009). Authors have classified various industrial services mainly into two categories:

services supporting the product and services supporting the client. Finally, based on these two categorizations, authors suggest possible paths a firm can follow for a smooth transition to hybrid value creation (e.g. More 2001; Penttinen and Palmer 2007; Matthyssens and Vandenbempt 2008, 2010). Research suggests that only after firms have mastered providing services related to their product should they experiment with services related to the customer. There is consensus in the literature that the transition to hybrid value creation is a medium- to long-term process. Most authors agree that resistance to change can be both internal, e.g. employees and external, e.g. customers.

*Table 9: Research on the innovation view*

| Sub-topic | Study focus | Study | Year | Type |
|---|---|---|---|---|
| **Innovation management** | Innovation dynamics in complex products | Miller et al. | 1995 | Case study |
| | Effects of product complexity on innovation process | Hobday | 1998 | Case study |
| | Challenges faced during execution of CoPS | Hansen and Rush | 1998 | Case study |
| | Technology management and problems faced | Hobday and Rush | 1999 | Theoretical |
| | Innovation in context of project-based, service-enhanced firms | Gann and Salter | 2000 | Theoretical |
| | Incumbents lack of interest in alternate uses of existing technology | Magnusson, Tell, and Watson | 2005 | Case study |
| | Integrated innovation vs. separated innovation in context of product-related services | Gebauer et al. | 2008 | Case study |
| | A customer perspective to develop successful integrated solutions | Brax and Jonsson | 2009 | Case study |
| | A service-centered perspective to develop successful integrated solutions | Windahl and Lakemond | 2010 | Case study |
| **Firms in and process for transition)** | A process to formulate product service strategies | Frambach, Wels-Lips, and Gündlach | 1997 | Case study |
| | Service strategies for manufacturing sector | Mathieu | 2001 | Theoretical |
| | A transition path with stages | More | 2001 | Case study |
| | Tools to think in the new paradigm of solutions | Berggren and Nacher | 2002 | Case study |
| | Importance of service-oriented management systems for the success of service strategies in industrial firms | Homburg, Faßnacht, and Günther | 2002 | Quantitative |
| | Incumbents reaction when they face competition from solution providers | Hardstone | 2004 | Case study |

| | | | |
|---|---|---|---|
| What is required to be successful in an extended service business in the context of manufacturing firms | Gebauer, Fleisch, and Friedli | 2005 | Case study |
| Effects of external environment on business strategy and success factors | Gebauer | 2007 | Quantitative |
| Two paths for a transition from a transaction based vendor to relationship based vendor | Penttinen and Palmer | 2007 | Case study |
| Service strategies for product manufacturing firms | Gebauer, Bravo-Sanchez, and Fleisch | 2008 | Case study |
| Cognitive biases and customer support services | Gebauer, Krempl, and Fleisch | 2008 | Case study |
| Proposes pathways and strategies for a transition from a product-based to a solutions-based strategy | Matthyssens and Vandenbempt | 2008 | Case study |
| An operations strategy for delivering product-centric service offerings | Baines et al. | 2009 | Case study |
| Firms need to align their product, service and organization to deliver successful PSS | Pawar, Beltagui, and Riedel | 2009 | Mixed methods |
| Identifies transition trajectories for moving into services | Matthyssens and Vandenbempt | 2010 | Case study |

## 3.6 The Business Level View

The business level view contains publications that have been clustered into three sub-groups: *'business models'*, *'viability in specific industries'*, and *'engineering and information technology'* (see *Table 10*).

*Business models* encompasses publications that have classified business models based on different characteristics and features. These include publications that have focused solely on categorizing downstream business models (e.g. Wise and Baumgartner 1999) or sustainable PSS (e.g. Roy 2000). Some authors have classified business models based on the targeted result; for example, an improvement in operating performance or an increase in asset effectiveness (e.g. Sharma and Molloy 1999). Others have based their categorization on extent of product and service content in such combinations. Here eight types of PSS are identified that are clustered into product-oriented, use-oriented or result-oriented business models (e.g. Tukker 2004). Analyzed publications also considered possible opportunities for firms to grow through services (e.g. Sawhney 2004; Raddats and Easingwood) depending on their position in the value chain (e.g. Gebauer, Paiola, and Edvardsson 2010). Despite these different categorization logics, there is no agreement or inclination towards any specific categorization logic.

*Viability in specific industries* contains publications that focus on checking the barriers and opportunities of specific product–service business models in various industries including construction, furniture, aerospace, machine tools, chemicals, and diagnostics. It is evident that drivers and barriers vary considerably in different industries.

*Engineering and information technology* contains publications that provide an engineering perspective on developing offerings. Also included are publications that focus on the use of IT architecture frameworks for designing hybrid value creation (e.g. Beverungen, Knackstedt, and Müller 2008; Thomas, Walter, and Loos 2008; Zellner 2008). In addition, there is research that deals with IT-supported customer services processes (e.g. Thomas and Nüttgens 2008). Research emphasizes that the use of information technology in hybrid offerings can help firms become more flexible and efficient in meeting customer demands.

*Table 10: Research on the business level view*

| Sub-topic | Study focus | Study | Year | Type |
|---|---|---|---|---|
| **Business models** | Framework to identify cost effective after-sales service strategies for different segments | Lele | 1997 | Theoretical |
| | Downstream business models | Wise and Baumgartner | 1999 | Case study |
| | Four sources of value creation | Sharma and Molloy | 1999 | Case study |
| | Sustainable PSS | Roy | 2000 | Case study |
| | Service opportunity matrix | Sawhney, Balasubramanian, and Krishnan | 2004 | Case study |
| | Eight different types of PSS clustered into three categories | Tukker | 2004 | Theoretical |
| | Four different service strategies for SMEs based on their position in the value chain | Gebauer, Paiola, and Edvardsson | 2010 | Case study |
| | Three supplier–customer constellations for different service strategies | Holmström, Brax, and Ala-Risku | 2010 | Conceptual |
| | Four different service strategies and three growth options through services for product-centric businesses | Raddats and Easingwood | 2010 | Case study |
| **Viability in specific industries** | Benefits of integrating diagnostic and pharmaceuticals | Gilham and Rowland | 2001 | Case study |
| | Innovation potential of integrated services for medium-sized construction contractors | Hartmann and Girmscheid | 2004 | Case study |
| | Integrated solutions for the construction industry | Brady, Davies, and Gann | 2005b | Exploratory interviews |

| | | | | |
|---|---|---|---|---|
| | Barriers and opportunities of PSS models for the furniture market | Besch | 2005 | Exploratory interviews |
| | Micro-factory retailing in automotive sector | Williams | 2006 | Case study |
| | Baby prams based on leasing and product remanufacturing | Mont, Dalhammar, and Jacobsson | 2006 | Case study |
| | Product life management in the aerospace industry | Ward and Graves | 2007 | Exploratory interviews |
| | Product-service con in aerospace, construction and engineering | Johnstone, Dainty, and Wilkinson | 2008 | Case study |
| | PSS business models in the b2b context for machine tools industry | Azarenko et al. | 2009 | Case study |
| | Integrating products and service in the aerospace industry | Johnstone, Dainty, and Wilkinson. | 2009 | Case study |
| | Realities of through-life value creation in the construction industry | Leiringer, Green, and Raja | 2009 | Case study |
| | PSS in chemical industry: five unique services | Anttonen | 2010 | Case study |
| | The case of a mobile sports companion as IT-supported product-service bundle | Leimeister, Knebel, and Krcmar | 2010 | Exploratory study |
| **Engineering and information technology** | A perspective for developing ERP systems to meet the demands of hybrid value creation | Becker et al. | 2008 | Theoretical |
| | Developing service oriented architectures for PSS | Beverungen, Knackstedt, and Müller | 2008 | Theoretical |
| | Breaking down solutions systematically into modules for repeatable solutions | Böhmann, Langer, and Schermann | 2008 | Theoretical |
| | Engineering perspective to design and develop product-service systems | Thomas, Walter, and Loos | 2008 | Case study |
| | Designing hybrid value creation by means of architectures | Zellner | 2008 | Case study |
| | Conceptual modeling for the development of PSS | Becker, Beverungen, and Knackstedt | 2010 | Theoretical |
| | Information technology for efficient customer service processes | Thomas and Nüttgens[#] | 2010 | Mixed methods |

[#] Thomas and Nüttigen are the editors of this book.

## 3.7 Sustainability Aspects

Sustainability is often related to the concept of dematerialization; i.e. the reduction in quantity of materials either absolutely or relatively to serve the economic function in the society. In addition to changing the competitive dynamics, sustainability is also considered as a goal of product-service combinations. The publications in this category have been split into two sub-groups: *'human behavior and consumption'* and *'evaluation of sustainability'* (see *Table 11*).

*Human behavior and consumption* contains publications that discuss the barriers posed by human behavior and habits for the acceptance of product-service combinations. Also, the question of how to influence human consumption habits is covered here (e.g. Meijkamp 1998). In addition, the acceptance of sharing business models by customers is delved into (e.g. Hirschl, Konrad, and Scholl. 2003; Mont 2004b). Current research also notes that social and socioeconomic considerations are often ignored when evaluating sustainability (e.g. Halme, Jasch, and Scharp 2004; Halme et al. 2006). There is an agreement in the analyzed publications that a substantial shift in human behavior is essential for the acceptance of sharing business models.

*Evaluation of sustainability* focuses on measuring sustainability goals from both a macro and a micro perspective. Also included are publications that evaluate the suitability of specific business models towards sustainability (e.g. Dobers and Wolff 1999). There are contrasting opinions regarding the viability of reaching sustainability goals through moving to a functional economy. Some authors insist that on a macro-level there is no reduction in material intensity when shifting from a manufacturing to a service-based economy (e.g. Jespersen 1999; Bartolomeo et al. 2003). In addition, there is considerable debate about whether business models based on sharing or joint use of assets have a positive effect on material intensity (i.e. reduction in material use). Authors suggest that dysfunctional human behavior may erode all possible sustainability gains made through the use of innovative product-service combinations.

*Table 11: Research on sustainability aspects*

| Sub-topic | Study focus | Study | Year | Type |
|---|---|---|---|---|
| **Human behavior and consumption** | Approach to change customer behavior | Meijkamp | 1998 | Quantitative |
| | Consumer openness to sharing models; four kinds of consumers identified | Hirschl, Konrad, and Scholl | 2003 | Case study |
| | Social or socioeconomic benefits are crucial aspects of sustainability | Halme, Jasch, and Scharp | 2004 | Theoretical |
| | What affects the acceptance of sharing models? | Mont | 2004b | Case study |
| | Social process and acceptance of Local Exchange Trading Systems (LETS) | Briceno and Stagl | 2006 | Quantitative |
| | Social benefits of sustainable home services and their acceptance | Halme et al. | 2006 | Quantitative |
| **Evaluation of sustainability** | Existing business models do not support dematerialization | Dobers and Wolff | 1999 | Theoretical |
| | Shift to a service economy does not have environmental benefits | Jespersen | 1999 | Quantitative |
| | Shift from products to services need not be eco-efficient | Bartolomeo et al. | 2003 | Theoretical |
| | Impact of sharing business models on environment | Mont | 2004c | Case study |
| | Intensity of material use in lease and reuse business models | Tasaki, Hashimoto, and Moriguchi | 2006 | Quantitative |

## 3.8 The Macroeconomic Perspective

This category contains publications that focus on the macroeconomic perspective of hybrid value creation. Publications have been broken down into two sub-groups: *'prevalence and effect'* and *'policy making'* (see *Table 12*).

*Prevalence and effect* consists of publications that explore how widespread hybrid value creation is (e.g. Stille 2003; Acha et al. 2004; Hornschild, Kinkel, and Lay 2004) and the financial impact of hybrid value creation on firm profitability (e.g. Fang, Palmatier, and Steenkamp 2008). Research shows that more and more firms from the developed economies are moving into hybrid value creation (e.g. Korte, Rijkers-Defranse, and Zweck 2009; Lay et al. 2010). Even though this is leading to an increase in overall sales (turnover), the profitability as a percentage of sales is actually decreasing (Neely 2008).

*Policy making* contains publications that look at how the state should contribute in promoting product-service combinations and incubating innovation (e.g. Davies and Brady 1998; Mont and Lindhqvist 2003; Ceschin and Vezzoli 2010). In addition, a model is proposed for the efficient transfer of knowledge from academia to industry (e.g. Cook, Bhamra, and Lemon 2006). Authors agree that there is a need for proactive policy making for the advancement of hybrid value creation from the side of the State.

*Table 12: Research on the macroeconomic perspective*

| Sub-topic | Study focus | Study | Year | Type |
|---|---|---|---|---|
| **Prevalence and effect** | Prevalence of product-related services in mechanical and electrical industries in Germany | Stille | 2003 | Quantitative |
| | Prevalence of CoPS in the UK | Acha et al. | 2004 | Quantitative |
| | Prevalence of product-related services in mechanical industry in Germany | Hornschild, Kinkel, and Lay | 2004 | Quantitative |
| | Effect of servitization on firm value | Fang, Palmatier, and Steenkamp | 2008 | Quantitative |
| | Exploring the financial consequences of the servitization of manufacturing | Neely | 2008 | Quantitative |
| | A survey on the state of change: solution providers in the German capital goods industry | Sturm and Bading | 2008 | Quantitative |
| | An overview of hybrid value creation research in Germany, EU and a few other countries | Korte, Rijkers-Defranse, and Zweck | 2009 | Mixed |
| | Extent of servitization in European manufacturing industries | Lay et al. | 2010 | Quantitative |
| **Policy making** | Role of public policy in influencing innovation in CoPS | Davies and Brady | 1998 | Case study |
| | Role of policy making for advancement of product service systems | Mont and Lindhqvist | 2003 | Narrative |
| | Transfer of knowledge from academia to manufacturing firms | Cook, Bhamra, and Lemon | 2006 | Case study |
| | Role of public policy in stimulating PSS innovation in the automotive industry | Ceschin and Vezzoli | 2010 | Narrative |

*Table 13* provides an overview of the roots for each of the eight research categories. It states where the publications come from in terms of geography (country), the outlet they are published in and the discipline they are rooted in.

*Table 13: An overview of roots for the eight research categories*

| **Area** | **Most prolific geographies (Number of papers)** | **Most prolific journal (s) (Number of papers)** | **Most contributions rooted in which discipline** |
|---|---|---|---|
| Strategic view | USA (7); UK (5); Germany (4); Sweden (2) | Journal of Service Management (3); Industrial Marketing Management (2) | Marketing, Strategy, Operations |
| Organization view | UK (11); USA (10); Switzerland (4); Germany, Sweden (3); Italy (2) | International Journal of Production Economics, International Journal of Service Industry Management, Journal of Manufacturing Technology Management; Journal of Service Research, Industrial Marketing Management, European Journal of Innovation Management (2) | Engineering, Operations, Innovation management |
| Marketing view | USA (8); Germany (7); Netherlands (2) | Controlling (3); McKinsey Quarterly, Journal of Marketing, Journal of Service Management, Journal of Manufacturing Technology Management (2) | Marketing, Strategy |
| Design view | UK (5); Denmark (4); Germany (2) | Journal of Cleaner Production (5); Journal of Manufacturing Technology (4); Journal of Engineering Design (2) | Engineering, Sustainability, Design sciences |
| Innovation view | UK (7); Switzerland (5); Canada, Finland, Netherlands (2) | Industrial Marketing Management (4); International Journal of Operations and Production Management (3); Industrial and Corporate Change, Research Policy (2) | Engineering, Innovation management, Operations |
| Business level view | UK (9); Germany (8); USA (4); Netherlands, Finland, Sweden (2) | Wirtschaftsinformatik (4); Journal of Cleaner Production (3), Business Strategy and The Environment, Managing Service Quality (2) | Engineering, Information systems, Strategy |
| Sustainability aspects | Sweden (3); Finland (2) | Journal of Cleaner Production (5); Business Strategy and The Environment, Ecological Economics (2) | Sustainability |
| Macroeconomic perspective | Germany (5); UK (4) | Journal of Cleaner Production (2) | Economics, Sustainability |

# 4 Discussion and Reflection

So far the presented literature review has delivered a state-of-the-art report and presented a concise set of definitions of key concepts. Based on the identified literature, it has also developed a preliminary categorization of the field. Overall, this research categorization assesses the contribution of 169 publications in the field by highlighting and analyzing their topical foci, theoretical and empirical findings as well as the methods used. It clearly shows key foci of research interests within the eight viewpoints of the conceptual framework, but also allows for the identification of research gaps within the different categories.

## 4.1 Research Gaps

Below some of the most pressing research gaps for each category are presented. Readers interested in researching one of the research gaps identified in each category are advised to read the publications listed from the respective category.

### 4.1.1 *The strategic view*

Extant research, albeit mostly anecdotally, endorses the view that hybrid value creation helps change the competitive dynamics of a firm by helping it better meet customer needs. Hence, future research, based on empirical evidence, should identify how and to what extent hybrid value creation changes the competitive dynamics of a firm. It would also be interesting to understand how competition reacts when a firm makes a foray into hybrid value creation.

### 4.1.2 *The organization view*

Even though there is extensive research on how internal processes, people, structures, and rewards interact with each other in the context of traditional offerings, it has not been adequately studied in the context of hybrid value creation. This needs to be understood, especially as current research confirms that organizational dynamics differ in the context of hybrid value creation. In particular, the extent of internal organizational change required should be studied.

### 4.1.3 *The marketing view*

Even though there is research on the topic of pricing in the context of hybrid value creation, it is still limited and inadequate. The process of how the value of hybrid offerings is calculated and communicated to customers is, however, very relevant and needs further research. Hence, research, either qualitative or quantitative, is required to identify a model that will guide firms quantify cost, price, and value of product-service offerings.

### 4.1.4 *The Design view*

Although the existing research agrees that design for product-service offerings differs from that for traditional standalone offerings, it is not evident how they differ. This needs to be clarified through future research. Moreover, research has also emphasized the importance of integrating various stakeholders in the design process of combined offerings. This leads to another interesting area for future research, i.e. how to integrate and moderate stakeholder interaction in the context of designing product-service offerings.

### 4.1.5 *The Innovation view*

Current research endorses the idea that innovation management in the context of hybrid value creation requires new procedures and processes. Given that relatively little is known about the earlier stages of the innovation process in this context, research is required on how firms can search for and select from various ideas for innovation to engage in hybrid value creation. In addition, innovation research is required that looks at hybrid value creation as a whole phenomenon. As currently, research is split into two independent steams: product innovation and service innovation.

### 4.1.6 *The Business level view*

Based on different characteristics and features, current research proposes various schemes for classifying hybrid value creation business models. However, what is missing and required is to identify key drivers for value creation for the different types of hybrid value creation business models. In a similar vein, research points out that the drivers and barriers for the success of hybrid value creation vary considerably from industry to industry. Hence, research is essential to understand the dynamics of hybrid value creation in different industries.

#### 4.1.7 *Sustainability aspects*

Extant research has identified humankind's hedonistic value as one of the biggest hurdles for the acceptance of product–service offerings in the business-to-customer sector. Even though there has been some research conducted to unravel this challenge, it is extremely limited. Hence, further research should continue to focus on how to overcome *'human craving for ownership'*.

#### 4.1.8 *The Macroeconomic perspective*

Research has pointed out that the State can play an important role in fostering hybrid value creation; further research should focus on to what extent and how exactly should the State go about fostering hybrid value creation. Research should also identify current policies and procedures that discourage the acceptance of hybrid value creation.

## 4.2 Additional Insights

The analysis of the contributions across the presented categories reveals additional insights in terms of the evolution of the research area and methods used. This section provides a discussion and reflects on these two aspects.

#### 4.2.1 *Evolution of the research area*

The interest in research on hybrid value creation has grown in number and quality over the last three decades. *Figure 4* provides the reader with an overview of how the research body dealing with this phenomenon has slowly but considerably grown.

Following Levitt's seminal paper, the publications of the 1980s primarily looked at combining products and services as a worthwhile strategy to change competitive dynamics. Here research focused on services as a one possible way to increase revenues and become less dependent on economic upturns for the sale of capital goods. By the late 1990s most authors agreed that hybrid value creation was not a myth, but a reality. They not only understood the logic behind hybrid value creation, but also encouraged firms to seriously consider combining products and services into seamless offerings. Research identified hybrid value creation as an effective strategy for firms, especially from the richer economies, to compete on a basis other than cost.

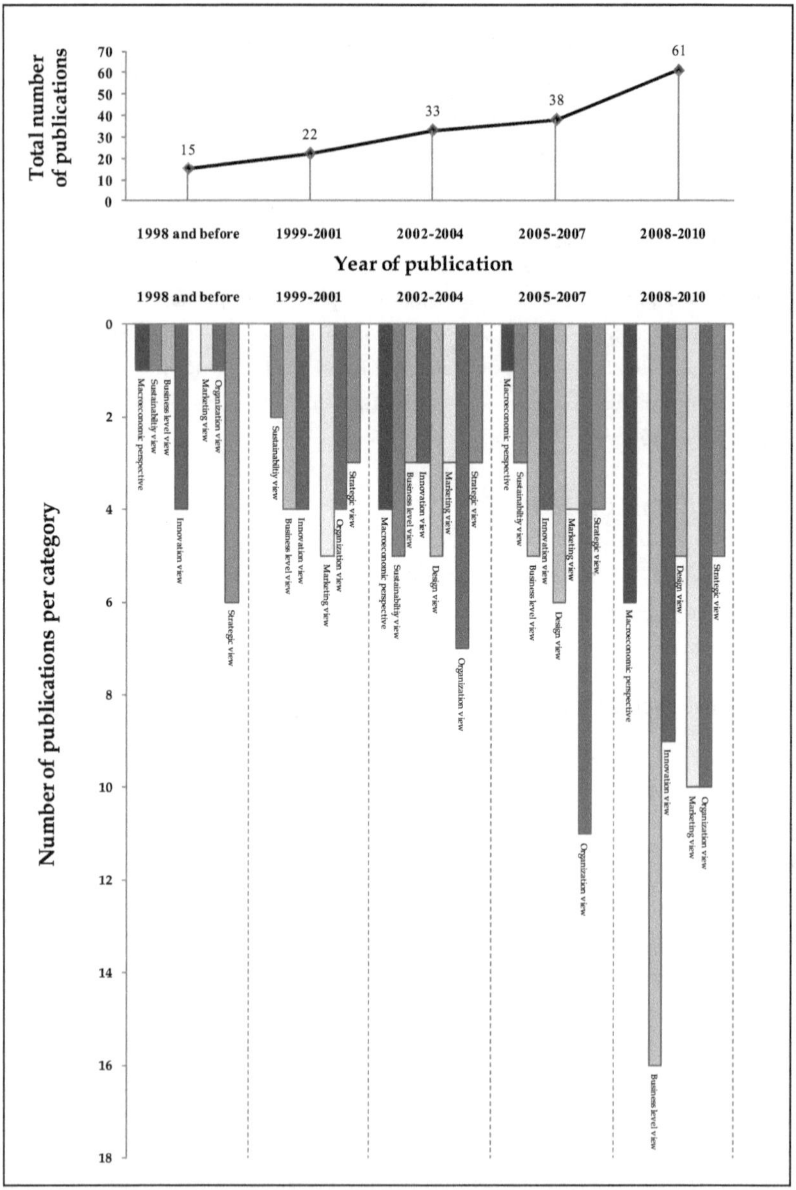


*Figure 4: Number of publications in total and for each research category*

Thus, it is not surprisingly that most research on hybrid value creation, even in 2010, originates from OECD countries (see *Table 13* for an overview of the countries with the highest number of contributions).

During this period (until 1998), *the strategic view* was the most important category as it supported and provided further impetus for manufacturing firms, who by then had begun to recognize the virtues of moving into services wholeheartedly. Simultaneously, in the late 1990s and early 2000s research also vigorously picked up the sustainability agenda. Around this time frame, most publications in the category *sustainability aspects* were published. Many publications advocated hybrid value creation as a strategy to reduce the negative environmental impact by meeting human needs innovatively. These two categories set the stage by establishing the logic behind hybrid value creation, but there was still limited research actually dealing with the issue of how to actually combine products and services.

This demand for research focusing on the intricacies of delivering successful product–service combinations was consequently met. This led to a steep rise in the number of publications in the following categories: *the organization view, the innovation view, the business level view,* and *the marketing view.* The most researched category is *the organization view* with over 30 publications that mainly dealt with new organizational forms and capabilities required for a successful entry into hybrid value creation. This has been ideally supported by an increase in publications in both *the innovation* and *business level views,* which further provided important pieces of the hybrid value creation puzzle. Publications from *the innovation view* provided crucial insights on transition paths firms could take from being a product-oriented firm to being a service-oriented firm. *The business level view* publications helped to get a grasp on different business models firms could choose from. Finally, the demand for research on pricing was met through the publications published in the last six years and assimilated in the category of *the marketing view.* Interestingly, firms have struggled with hybrid value creation and have identified design as a crucial success factor. Not surprisingly, firms are curious to learn about design in the context of product–service combinations. Consequently, scholars are starting to cross disciplines in order to learn how to actually support firms in their endeavor to design product–service combinations. Since 2002 research focusing solely on designing product–service combinations has been conducted, this has been clustered into *the design view* category.

### 4.2.2 *Methods used*

Qualitative research is the dominant research method used in the field of hybrid value creation so far. Since the phenomenon of hybrid value creation is relatively new, a preference towards qualitative research is understandable because it allows for deeper insights in the phenomenon under study by considering context-specific factors, labyrinthine patterns and casual relationships. Thus, it allows for the discovery and generation of theory in a context where relatively little is known about the underlying phenomenon (Eisenhardt 1989; Miles and Huberman 1994).

## 4.3 Dominant Directions for Future Research

A content analysis and confrontation of research results across the presented research categories identifies dominant strategic directions for future research on both a micro and macro level.

### 4.3.1 *Micro level*

Despite the broad range of available research on organizational design aspects, pricing and even business model categories, the work on hybrid value creation so far has not come to grips with the value creating attributes in hybrid offerings. Consequently, a clear understanding of the business models that could realize positive value creation is still missing on business unit and firm level. To fill this gap, a systematic integration of the diverse value creating concepts from the presented literature would be a valuable first step. A systematic empirical assessment would have to follow. In sum, despite the rich research efforts taking place worldwide and the broad range of results that has been integrated and presented in this review, knowledge on the value creation aspects of hybrid value creation are still scarce.

### 4.3.2 *Macro level*

The lack of knowledge and understanding in this area of the productivity and performance impact of hybrid value creation on the micro level is mirrored on the macro level. As already stated, the arguments underpinning the increasing popularity of hybrid value creation are manifold. In general, they include positive connotations as well as expectations about the economic impact of hybrid value creation. Across all categories, research widely underpins these expectations with theoretic reasoning, qualitative case illustrations as well as partial quantitative analyses. In this context of unanimity, Neely (2008) confronts the research community with an analysis of data from the OSIRIS database on 10,028 firms incorporated in 25 different countries which suggests that "while the manufacturing firms that have servitized are larger than traditional manufacturing firms in terms of sales revenues, at the aggregate level they also generate lower profits as a % of sales". This result can (and maybe should) be interpreted as a "wake-up call" for the international community of researchers to dig deeper into the productivity and performance impact of different types of hybrid value creation and their implementation strategies across industries and national boundaries.

# 5 Conclusion of the Review

This review brings together scattered research on the phenomenon of combining products and services into one document. It reveals that research on joint offerings of product and services has grown considerably in the last few years. However, the research body continues to be fragmented into different streams, which has understandably hampered academic exchange between researchers to an extent. Research published in the last two to three years has rectified this problem at least to some degree, as researchers from different strands are interchanging and using more than one term in a publication. Nonetheless, *product service systems* continues to be the dominant strand of research and this term today is extensively used in engineering, operations, information systems, design and sustainability disciplines.

Given the importance and the inherent complexity of the phenomenon 'hybrid value creation', the categorization presented in this review aims to assist the audience in benefitting from a systematic overview of the numerous publications in this research area. It sums up the research done in each of these categories and guides readers to important research gaps in each of these categories. Finally, it identifies two dominant strategic directions for future research:

1. Studies on understanding what really creates value in different product-service offerings on a micro level;
2. Studies on the productivity and performance impact of hybrid value creation on a macro level.

This dissertation chooses the first strategic direction of research and focuses on understanding what really creates value in different hybrid value creation business models.

This leads to the research question "how and where is value created in the different business models of hybrid value creation", which is tackled in detail in part III of this dissertation, *"Empirical study 1: The four clusters of hybrid value creation"*. In this study, four clusters of hybrid value creation are developed and the role and impact of four value creating attributes - identified from literature - for each cluster is empirically deducted.

# III

## Empirical Study 1:
## The Four Clusters of
## Hybrid Value Creation

# 1 Need and Goals

The systematic literature review (part II) identified that the field of hybrid value creation, despite the broad range of available research, has not come to grips with the value creating attributes in different hybrid offerings. As a result, even though firms have identified the potential of hybrid value creation, they are still not sure what factors really create value in different hybrid value creation business models. Not surprisingly, this challenge has been also identified as a dominant research gap in the systematic literature review.

This leads to the research question of this empirical study[4], which is to gain a better understanding of how and where value is created in different business models of hybrid value creation. To close this gap, this study investigates 80 successful offerings of hybrid value creation and provides an organizational perspective to this challenge. The case vignettes of these 80 offerings can be found on the online database on the website www.hybridvaluecreation.com (for more information on the database and website see *Annex A: Technical Document – www.hybridvaluecreation.com*).

To reach the goals of this study, first, value creating attributes need to be identified. It must be noted that extant literature only sporadically mentions different value creating attributes, but does not consolidate them. Second, different clusters[5] of hybrid value creation business models need to be developed. This is required because product–service combinations range from simple delivery services to complex turnkey products. Without this second step the impact of this study would diminish as it does not make sense, for example, to compare a car rental service with a complex mass transport solution. Once this is done, the role and impact of the identified value creating attributes on the developed clusters of hybrid value creation is deducted. Finally, the key value creating attribute for each cluster is identified. Hence the goals of this study are summarized as:

1. To identify and bring together diverse value creating attributes from extant literature;
2. To develop different clusters of hybrid value creation business models;

---

[4] Note that an earlier version of this research was presented at *Multikonferenz Wirtschaftsinformatik* (MKWI) 2010, Göttingen and published as Velamuri, Neyer, and Möslein 2010. Although that publication was co-authored, the identification of relevant theory, the research design, the collection of data, the analysis of data, and the interpretation of results are primarily attributable to Vivek K. Velamuri.

[5] A cluster consists of hybrid value creation business models that are similar to each other.

3. To deduct the role and impact of the identified value creating attributes on the developed clusters of hybrid value creation;
4. To identify key value creating attribute for each cluster.

The remainder of this empirical study is organized as follows. Chapter 2 identifies four value creating attributes from extant literature. Chapter 3 explains the method used and how four different clusters of hybrid value creation business models are developed. Chapter 4 describes the role and impact of the identified value creating attributes for each of developed case clusters. Chapter 5 provides the results. Chapter 6 summarizes this study and concludes by identifying two clusters – *embedded products* and *solutions* – that require further research.

# 2 Four Value Creating Attributes

A cross analysis of the publications from the systematic literature review (169 publications in eight categories) identifies four distinct value creating attributes in the field of hybrid value creation. These are:

1. Individualization (e.g. Davies, Brady, and Hobday 2007)
2. Marketing-integration (e.g. Foote et al. 2001)
3. Operational-integration (e.g. Johansson, Krishnamurthy, and Schlissberg 2003)
4. Firm–customer interaction (e.g. Phillips, Ochs, and Schrock,1999)

In this chapter, these four value creating attributes and their roots in previous publications are explained. For this purpose, some additional publications (not part of the systematic literature review) were also identified, which support the value creating potential of the four value creating attributes.

## 2.1 Individualization

Individualization (also referred to as customization or personalization) is identified as a value creating attribute in literature. Its role as a value driver is derived from the fact that customers are willing to pay a price premium for an individualized offering (Hart 1996; Kotha 1996; Piller, Möslein, and Stotko 2004; Broekhuizen and Alsem 2000). There are two reasons for this:

1. Any increase in interaction between the customer and the supplier that is positively perceived by the customer (Franke and Piller 2003);
2. Any increase in utility a customer perceives from the individualized product that meets his/her needs better than other standard offers available on the market (Chamberlain 1962).

In hybrid value creation literature there is agreement that individualization is one the most important value creating attributes (Mont 2002a; Davies, Brady, and Hobday 2006; Bonnemeier et al. 2008; Davies, Brady, and Hobday 2007; Hax and Wilde 1999; Krishnamurthy, Johansson, and Schlissberg 2003). Also compared to pure products, combined offerings have more avenues for differentiation as they contain services which can be easily customized in many unique ways to meet the exact requirements of customers (MacMillan and McGrath 1997).

Even though individualization has been identified as a value creating attribute, literature also provides a cautious note on the dangers of *over individualization*. Research advocates finding the right balance between the level of standardization and individualization (Davies, Brady, and Hobday 2006). The art is to develop standardized solution ready components which can be combined to provide a range of customized offerings to meet the exact needs of different customers (Page and Siemplenski 1983; Davies and Brady 2000; Foote et al. 2001). Davies, Brady, and Hobday state that

> *"If systems sellers develop a comprehensive options list of standardized components, each configuration can be a unique, customized solution. The solution to customer's needs is a customized adaptation of the basic modular system and its standardized components. Component standardization allows the vendor to benefit from economies of scale in production, while providing each customer with a system configuration 'as though it were produced on a job-shop basis'"* (2007: 186).

The degree of individualization may vary from customer-specific individualization, as in the case of individualized Bentley cars, to segment-specific individualizations as provided by 3M for eleven specific industries (Krishnamurthy, Johansson, and Schlissberg 2003; Sawhney 2006).

This study will identify which part of combined offerings is individualized in the selected cases.

## 2.2 Marketing-Integration

Integration is the degree to which various components of an offering (i.e. products and services) are combined or interrelated to deliver value beyond the sum of the included components (Shepherd and Ahmed 2000; Foote et al. 2001; Johansson, Krishnamurthy, and Schlissberg 2003; Doster and Roegner 2005). Integration can be broken down into two distinct value creating attributes which are:

1. Marketing-integration – also known as commercial integration;
2. Operational-integration – also known as technical-integration.

Marketing-integration is about delivering value to customers by combining various components, which can be acquired by the customer separately, into a single transaction (Sawhney 2006; Bonnemeier et al. 2008; Krishnamurthy, Johansson, and Schlissberg 2003). In the words of Sawhney:

> *"Marketing integration refers to integration across the entire decision-making and buying cycle, from the pre-sales search to post-sales service and support. Marketing integration is temporal in nature, because it spans the sequence of steps that customers go through in searching, evaluating, buying, installing, using, servicing and maintaining a system of products. Customers may benefit from being able to search a single location for all elements of the solution, to buy all products and services they need from a 'one-stop-shop' provider, pay a single bundled price for the solution, have a single provider to install and deploy the solution, call a single number for customer support and service, and maintain a single vendor relationship"* (Sawhney 2006: 369).

Marketing-integration also allows the customer to benefit from consolidated vendor accountability. That is, if there is a problem (for example, an agreed upon service level agreement not being met), the customer is offered, so to say, a throat to choke (Johansson, Krishnamurthy, and Schlissberg 2003).

This study will identify what kind of marketing-integration is exhibited in the selected cases.

## 2.3 Operational-Integration

The third value generating component is known as operational-integration. Research suggests that operational-integration is the value creating attribute that differentiates a bundle from a true combined offering (Johansson, Krishnamurthy, and Schlissberg 2003; Sawhney 2006). It is about seamlessly linking and/or engineering the various components of an offering into an operational system (Möslein, Adamczyk, and Velamuri 2010; Buriánek et al. 2007; Windahl et al. 2004). Johansson, Krishnamurthy, and Schlissberg state that

> *"technical integration links the elements of the offer functionally – it makes the components of a given system interoperable – to create extra value: the parts snap together in beneficial ways, enabling vendors to charge a premium"* (2003: 119).

Sawhney supports them by stating that

> *"Operational integration may mean that individual products are engineered to work better together, or that individual services are delivered using an integrated platform. The value of operational-integration depends on two main factors – the effort that customers would need to expend to integrate the products and solutions themselves and the value that they place on their time. If the individual products are standardized (e.g., the components of a personal computer), integration is not difficult and customer would place less value on the integration"* (Sawhney 2006: 370).

Such offerings save customers' effort and time by pre-combining the various elements into the desired solution. On top, they also mitigate customers' risk by shifting the complications involved in operational-integration to the supplier. Hobday, Davies, and Prencipe (2005) suggest that system integration has evolved beyond its original technical task (of seamlessly integrating various components) to become a strategic business dimension.

This study will identify what kind of operational-integration is provided in the selected cases.

## 2.4 Firm–Customer Interaction

Firm–customer interaction is the fourth crucial value creating attribute of hybrid value creation. It captures the relationship (and interaction) between a customer and a supplier that creates value (Grönroos 2000; Möslein, Adamczyk, and Velamuri 2010). Webster (1992) views firm–customer relationships as a key strategic resource for a business. He emphasizes the need to change the dynamics of firm–customer interaction from a transaction-based to one based on relationship. Firm–customer interaction is crucial to better understand customer needs. This in turn is required for effective customization, marketing-integration and operational-integration to take place. For a firm, the basis of competitive advantage has shifted from delivering a salable product (traditional) to its ability to flow new technology into its subsystems and rapidly tailor them to the meet unique needs of individual customers (Phillips, Ochs, and Schrock 1999). Interestingly, a study on industrial purchasing has highlighted that satisfaction from the purchase process, i.e. pre-sale services such as consulting, is more likely to persuade the customer to buy future products from the same supplier than the satisfaction the customer gets from the product itself (Tanner 1996).

Even though many levels of firm–customer relationship intensity (length/duration and breadth/scope) exist, this study categorizes all relationships into one of the two ends of the continuum. They are classified as either:

1. *Transaction-based interaction* is a onetime interaction between the economic actors involved in a transaction. Money is paid in exchange for a product and/or service in a single transaction.
2. *Relationship-based interaction* is more intense than a repeated transaction-based interaction. It is about regular interaction between the supplier and the customer, where both parties benefit from each other's knowledge and understand each other's problems and concerns.

This study will identify what kind of firm–customer interaction is exhibited in the selected cases. In addition, revenue models are also simultaneously studied as they provide a good proxy to understand firm–customer interaction (Velamuri, Neyer, and Möslein 2008). Upfront revenue models indicate a transaction-based firm–customer interaction. Revenue models with periodic payments - for example, weekly, monthly, quarterly or yearly invoices - indicate a relationship-based firm–customer interaction.

The role and impact of these four value creating attributes for different hybrid value creating offerings is developed in chapter 4, but prior to that chapter 3 explains how and why the four clusters of hybrid value creation business models are developed.

# 3 Method and Data

The need to develop different clusters of hybrid value creation business models arises because it does not make sense to compare two completely distinct product-service offerings, for example, a game console and a laundry solution, with each other. Hence this chapter, in addition to explaining the research method, explains how four distinct clusters of hybrid value creation are developed.

This chapter contains three sections. The first section explains why the qualitative case study method is used. The second section describes the research approach in detail. This includes how the case studies were identified and four different clusters of hybrid value creation developed. Finally, the third section deals with data, i.e. the case studies split into the four clusters in detail.

## 3.1 Research Design

Since relatively little is known about what creates value in various hybrid value creation offerings, an explorative qualitative research is chosen. Compared to a quantitative research approach, qualitative data gives deep insights in the phenomenon under study by considering context-specific factors, complex patterns, and causal relationships. Thus, qualitative research allows discovering and generating theory in a context when relatively little is known about the underlying phenomenon (Eisenhardt 1989; Miles and Huberman 1994).

In line with this an exploratory case study with embedded units of analysis was conducted (Eisenhardt 1989; Yin 2003). To strengthen the resulting interferences a comparative case study is applied, i.e. data from several cases was gathered and examined in an iterative way (Yin 2003). The iterative process of analyzing within-case and cross-case data supported the creation of new relationships and aimed at the exploration of theoretical explanations for the phenomenon under study (Eisenhardt 1989).

## 3.2 Research Approach

The risk of learning from unsuccessful offerings is high as the determinants of failure are not yet well understood. Hence, for this study only successful cases were selected. For this, the selection was limited to examples that have been identified as successful in existing hybrid value creation literature (both academic and industry publications were taken into consideration).

In these publications, product–service offerings are defined as successful when they lead to:

1. A competitive advantage and/or
2. Increased customer loyalty and/or
3. Increase in revenues and/or
4. An economically viable environmental benefit.

A starting point for this was to identify instances that could be developed into cases (an overview of steps involved in this research approach is presented in *Figure 5*).

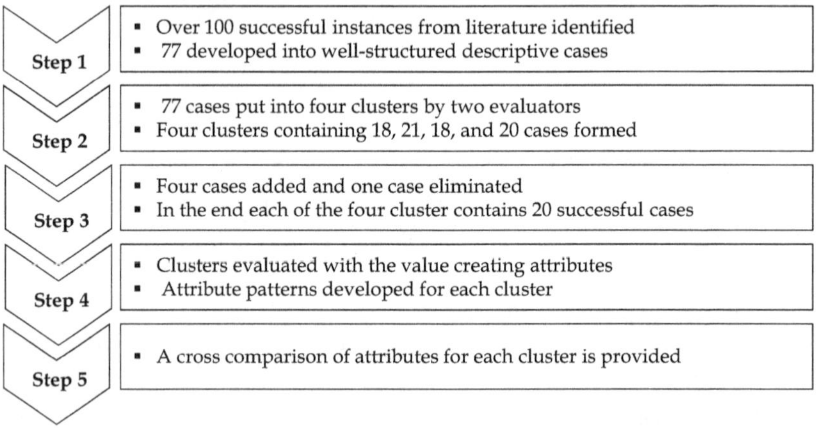


*Figure 5: Overview of research approach – empirical study 1*

Most instances were identified from academic literature (i.e. journal papers, dissertations, and working papers). For this the principal research-databases were searched using key terms such as business-related services, complex product systems, customer solutions, dematerialization, full service, functional products, hybrid offerings, integrated solutions, product service bundles, product service systems, product-related services, and servitization. To this, instances that came up in industry and consultancy reports and articles were added. These were identified using *Google Scholar* as they were beyond the scope of the research-databases.

In total over 100 instances were identified. Out of these 77 could be developed into well-structured one-page descriptive cases based on interviews and/or openly available company information. The remaining instances were excluded because data on some crucial aspects was not available. After reading the structured case descriptions, the 77 cases were grouped - with the help of a second evaluator - into four clusters based on their primary goal. The four clusters formed can be described as follows:

1. *Embedded products*: contains case studies where the primary goal is to create a new offering or protect an existing product from competition by enhancing it with embedded services using digital technologies (e.g. ergo meters embedded with personal trainer software);
2. *Leasing/ renting/ sharing/ pooling (from now on termed "leasing & co."):* contains case studies where the primary goal is to expand the market for capital intensive (sometimes relative) products by providing them to customers on rental- or use-basis (e.g. car sharing);
3. *Mass customization:* contains case studies where the primary goal is to provide individualized products to end customers at a reasonable premium (e.g. customized shoes);
4. *Solutions:* contains case studies where the primary goal is to help customers focus on their core competencies instead of worrying about aspects such as asset availability (e.g. facility management).

The four clusters contained 18, 21, 18, and 20 cases respectively. To have clusters with an equal number of cases, four cases identified through the internet were added and one case was eliminated.[6] This meant that, in the end, each of the four clusters contained 20 cases. This clustering emerged as an obvious step in the research process because directly comparing individual cases from different clusters would be a futile process.

Next the four clusters (80 cases in total) were evaluated, again with the help of a second evaluator, on the four value creating attributes - namely, individualization, marketing-integration, operational-integration, firm–customer interaction - described in the previous chapter. For evaluation, a description for each category in each case is preferred to using a numeric or continuum-based scale (e.g. high to low). This study explicitly identified:

1. What part of an offering is individualized?
2. What kind of marketing-integration is found?

[6] The cases that were added or eliminated did not affect the characteristics of any cluster. This step was solely taken to have four clusters with equal number of cases.

3. What type operational-integration is evident?
4. What kind of firm–customer interaction is visible?

In a few instances (fewer than 5%) the evaluators disagreed on an evaluation. Such instances were discussed until an agreement was reached between the evaluators.

Finally, each of the four case clusters is analyzed individually and clear attribute patterns are developed for each cluster. Later, a cross comparison of the attributes for each cluster is provided.

## 3.3 Introduction: The Four Clusters of Hybrid Value Creation

In this section, a theoretical introduction to the four clusters of hybrid value creation is provided. They are also examined to see if they meet the hybrid value creating criteria as defined previously in part I. The 20 identified cases in each cluster are also listed.

*Table 14: The four clusters based on goals*

| Cluster | Description | Aspect of Hybridism | Aspect of Value creation |
|---|---|---|---|
| **Embedded products** | Embedded products are offerings where traditional or new services are embedded in the product using digital technologies to enhance the offering. | Service is embedded in the product. | Empirical evidence available from qualitative case research such as GMs Onstar (Slywotzky and Wise 2003), Apple's iPod and iTunes offering (Auguste, Harmon, and Pandit 2006) or Adidas MiCoach (Möslein and Velamuri 2009). |
| **Leasing & Co.** | These business models do not aim to sell the product, but the product is made available to the user via leasing & co. Products are sometimes shared by a number of users. | Product is offered as a service. | Reduced capital investment as well as repair and maintenance costs on the side of the customer (Tukker 2004). |
| **Mass Customi-zation** | Mass customization is about providing individualized products or services to customers. | Customization is the service that is performed on the product. | Additional utility perceived by the customer in a mass customized product compared to available alternatives (Piller, Möslein, and Stotko 2004). |
| **Solutions** | Solutions are seamless offerings of products and services that meet specific customer needs. | The service is about integrating and customizing the offering. | Value generation through level of customization and integration (Krishnamurthy, Johansson, and Schlissberg 2003). |

It must be noted that a case study coming from any specific cluster may contain elements from another cluster. For example, a case in that is categorized under 'solutions' may contain some elements of the 'leasing & co.' or 'embedded products' clusters. *Table 14* provides a summary of this section.

### *3.3.1 Embedded products*

Embedded products are offerings where traditional or new services are embedded in the product using new digital technologies. The primary goal is to either create a radically new offering or protect an existing product by improving the perceived use value of it. Sawhney, Balasubramanian, and Krishnan describe such offerings as spatial expansion to adjacent value chains by embedding service elements into hardware. They state that

> *"the search for spatial expansion opportunities begins with the identification of promising 'pivot points' in current activities and capabilities that can lead to involvement with customers in other areas and continues with the identification of platforms or brands that can support new services"* (Sawhney, Balasubramanian, and Krishnan 2004: 38).

They described GM's OnStar platform which provides emergency services as a successful embedded service. A couple of other successful examples of such embedded services are Apple's iPod and iTunes offering (Auguste, Harmon, and Pandit 2006) and Adidas MiCoach (Möslein and Velamuri 2009).

*The 20 cases from the 'embedded product' cluster:*

All 20 cases contained in this cluster are from the b2c sector. The cluster includes both enhanced and radically new offerings. They are listed in *Table 15*.

*Table 15: List of embedded product cases*

| | | | |
|---|---|---|---|
| ▪ Diabetes monitor | ▪ Fitness machine II | ▪ Mobile phone | ▪ Personal trainer II |
| ▪ e-book reader | ▪ Gaming console | ▪ Music player, trainer & community | ▪ Personal trainer III |
| ▪ Emergency services | ▪ Handheld gaming device | ▪ Music player & online store | ▪ Physical activity monitor |
| ▪ Electricity monitor | ▪ Home control system | ▪ Navigation system | ▪ Programmable toy |
| ▪ Fitness machine I | ▪ Internet table-radio | ▪ Personal trainer I | ▪ Web-based personal trainer |

*Does the cluster of embedded products meet the criteria of hybrid value creation?*

The hybrid aspect of embedded products is clearly visible as the service is often embedded in the product or augmented by an online portal that either sells add-ons or provides further products as services.

Value creation is more challenging to judge, as it is not easy to verify whether the providers of embedded products charge a premium. However, there is evidence in at least some of the cases that customers are willing to pay for the additional service attached. For example, GM's OnStar platform services have been a huge success with over two million service subscribers paying in 2001 (Slywotzky and Wise 2003). Another obvious example of a success story is Apple's music download service iTunes integrated with product offering iPod.

As embedded products meet both the criteria - hybridism and value creation - they are correctly called a cluster of hybrid value creation.

### 3.3.2 *Leasing & co.*

All four models - leasing/renting/sharing/pooling - have been classified under use-oriented product service systems (Tukker 2004). He states that

> *"the traditional product still plays a central role, but the business model is not geared towards selling products. The product stays in ownership with the provider, and is made available in a different form, and sometimes shared by a number of users"* (Tukker 2004: 248).

They have also been called *"shared utilization services"* where the aim is to increase the utilization of a product by sharing it between more users (Roy 2000). Such joint use is expected to be more environmentally sustainable as it leads to a reduction in the quantity of materials (either absolutely or relatively) while serving the same economic function in society (Mont 2004c).

*The 20 cases from the 'leasing & co.' cluster:*

Today, leasing & co. business models have expanded from the traditional lending libraries and rental car companies to many other consumer goods. The 20 cases, which come from both the business-to-business and the business-to-customer sectors, are listed in *Table 16*.

*Table 16: List of leasing & co. cases*

| | | | |
|---|---|---|---|
| ▪ Art pieces<br>▪ Baby prams<br>▪ Car rental<br>▪ Car sharing<br>▪ City bikes | ▪ Conference room sharing<br>▪ Copy machines<br>▪ DIY tools rental<br>▪ DVDs through post<br>▪ IT infrastructure | ▪ Luxury bags<br>▪ Mobile toilets<br>▪ Party equipment<br>▪ Personal office space<br>▪ Pet dogs | ▪ Resort property<br>▪ Trucks & moving equipment<br>▪ Wedding dress (ball dresses)<br>▪ White goods<br>▪ Yacht sharing |

*Does the cluster of leasing & co. meet the criteria of hybrid value creation?*

The hybrid aspect in leasing & co. is met as the product is provided as a service. To answer the value creation aspect, the evolution of book libraries serves as an example.

Before the advent of profit seeking lending libraries, in England in the eighteenth century, only the wealthy purchased books (Varian 2000). After such libraries opened, the demand for books greatly increased as the middle class also became customers of books, albeit on a rental basis. The rental business model made books affordable to the middle class. These new customers were willing to pay rent for a service (premium) which they would not have otherwise availed. This allowed the producers (publishing houses) to cater to a market that would have otherwise been ignored (Varian 2000). He also states that renting as a business model is viable when the marginal cost or production of a single copy is higher than the transactional costs of sharing the exemplar for which he provides the example of rental car market. In the context of hybrid value creation, customers are willing to pay a premium for the following two reasons:

1. they do not need to make a capital investment;
2. repair and maintenance is shifted back to the producer.

Examining the car rental industry, one can notice that the automobile companies appreciate the rental and lease market since it expands their customer base. The rental companies, next in line, obviously make a profit otherwise they would not exist. At the end of the value chain are customers who are paying rent (premium) for the use of a car. Hence this cluster is rightly classified as a cluster of hybrid value creation.

### 3.3.3 *Mass customization*

The term mass customization was coined by Davis. He states that:

> *"Mass Customization of markets means that the same large number of customers can be reached as in mass markets of the industrial economy, and simultaneously they can be treated individually as in the customized markets of pre-industrial economies"* (Davis 1987: 169).

A more practical definition is that

> *"Mass customization relates to the ability to provide individually designed products and services to every customer through high process flexibility and integration"* (Silveira, Borenstein, and Fogliatto 2001: 1).

In lay terms, mass customization is about providing products or services that meet specific customer needs, but without charging an exorbitant price premium for the delivered product or service.

*The 20 cases from the 'mass customization' cluster:*

All 20 cases contained in this cluster are from the b2c sector. A diverse range of mass customized products has been selected for this study. They are listed in *Table 17.*

*Table 17: List of mass customization cases*

| | | | |
|---|---|---|---|
| ▪ Customized beer labels | ▪ Customized handbags | ▪ Customized novels | ▪ Customized sofa covers |
| ▪ Customized breakfast cereal | ▪ Customized jams | ▪ Customized picture frames | ▪ Customized stationery |
| ▪ Customized coffee | ▪ Customized jeans | ▪ Customized shoes I | ▪ Customized t-shirts |
| ▪ Customized dolls | ▪ Customized lamps | ▪ Customized shoes II | ▪ Customized wedding rings |
| ▪ Customized golf balls | ▪ Customized liqueur | ▪ Customized snowboards | ▪ Customized wheel rims |

*Does the cluster of mass customization meet the criteria of hybrid value creation?*

There is enough evidence in the literature that customers are often willing to pay a premium for a customized product (Piller, Möslein, and Stotko 2004; Hart 1996; Piller and Franke 2004). This price premium (or willingness to pay) is based on the additional utility a customer perceives in a customized product compared to a non-customized product. It is reasonable to assume that extra costs incurred for the customization are covered in the price premium. Otherwise, mass customization would be a value destroyer.

The next part is to check the hybridism aspect, i.e. do they contain both product and service components. It is argued that for all mass customized products - for example, a mass customized chair or a pair of shoes - the service part is inseparable from the final product. The price premium, charged by the company and paid by the customer, is for the additional service in the form of customization that is conducted on the product. In contrast, mass customized services (e.g. a haircut) even though they create value, would not be considered as hybrid because they lack the product aspect.

As both criteria are met, mass customization (of products only) is also correctly called a cluster of hybrid value creation.

### 3.3.4 *Solutions*

Solutions have been defined as seamless offerings of products and services that meet customers' individual needs (Sharma and Molloy 1999; Wise and Baumgartner 1999; Foote et al. 2001; Bennett, Sharma, and Tipping 2001; Windahl et al. 2004; Davies 2004; Tuli, Kohli, and Bharadwaj 2007). It has been noticed that companies that come from both a product base (Foote et al. 2001) as well as a service base (Davies 2004) are changing their strategies from providing standalone products or services to providing solutions by integrating various products and services.

*The 20 cases from the 'solutions' cluster:*

All 20 cases contained in this cluster are from the b2b sector. They have been selected from a diverse range of industries. They are listed in *Table 18*.

*Table 18: List of solution cases*

| | | | |
|---|---|---|---|
| ▪ Aircraft engines<br>▪ Automation solutions<br>▪ Coffee machines<br>▪ Communication network solutions<br>▪ Crane solutions | ▪ Earthmoving equipment<br>▪ Elevator solutions<br>▪ Engineering machinery<br>▪ Facility management<br>▪ Fleet management | ▪ Green space management<br>▪ Healthcare solutions<br>▪ Heating solutions<br>▪ Integrated pest management<br>▪ Laundry solutions | ▪ Mass transport solutions<br>▪ Solar energy services<br>▪ Construction Industry<br>▪ Tool management<br>▪ Warehouse trucks |

*Does the cluster of solutions meet the criteria of hybrid value creation?*

Various definitions of solutions make it amply clear that solutions comprise both tangible and intangible components. Hence the hybrid aspect is clear. The next part is to check the value creation aspect.

To provide solutions one may need to expand vertically in the industry value chain (Davies 2004) or in other words it may be necessary to merge supplier and customer operations (Foote et al. 2001). However, for value creation the critical question is not which, but how various components are combined/integrated (Johansson, Krishnamurthy, and Schlissberg 2003; Sawhney 2006). Sawhney (2006) defined solutions as,

> *"an integrated combination of products and services customized for a set of customers that allows customers to achieve better outcomes than the sum of individual components of the solution"* (Sawhney 2006: 369).

Authors agree that the value in solutions is generated by the prevalence of individualization and integration (Möslein, Adamczyk, and Velamuri 2010; Krishnamurthy, Johansson, and Schlissberg 2003).

As solutions meet both the criteria - hybridism and value creation - they are rightly called a cluster of hybrid value creation.

# 4 Case Analysis

In the following, the role and impact of the value creating attributes - individualization, marketing-integration, operational-integration, and firm-customer interaction - for each of the four identified case clusters is described in detail.

## 4.1 Embedded Products

In all 20 cases of this cluster the main offering is standard. This does not mean that there is no individualization involved, but rather the initiative to individualize is handed back to the customer. Two main ways of doing this are observed:

1. The software-based service embedded in the product is individualizable by the customers themselves, e.g., *personal trainers* are embedded with a software program. These can be used to design individualized training plans to meet all of the customer's training requirements, from running a marathon to just keeping fit and healthy.
2. The supplier offered a wide range of further products as a service. The customer can pick and choose from this wide range at an extra cost, e.g., the *mobile device* provides a wide range of additional applications (apps) that can be purchased and downloaded. Similarly, the *e-book reader* is complemented with an online store that sells books in electronic versions.

Marketing-integration is noticed in nearly all the cases, but is mainly limited to the presence of online stores with additional offerings. Some also actively created communities of practice, as a service, for the customers to benefit from. This made sense especially in offerings in preventive healthcare (and in addition the *programmable toys*) where customers have common goals (for example weight reduction) or a need to get peer feedback and/or recognition for their efforts. Only two cases exhibited no marketing-integration.

Operational-integration is observed in all 20 cases. In all the cases it is in the form of high to extremely high levels of technical-integration of hardware and software components (in some cases the online store).

Firm–customer interaction, in all but one case, is transactional in nature. Firms continue to market embedded products as standalone products. This is also noticed by the fact that they continue to use upfront revenue models, i.e. the customer paid a final exchange value at the time of purchase. The only exception, which had a relationship-based firm–customer interaction, used a subscription revenue model (see *Table 19*).

*Table 19: Data analysis –'embedded products' cluster*

| Embedded Products | Type of individualization | Marketing-integration | Operational-integration | Firm–customer interaction |
|---|---|---|---|---|
| Diabetes monitor | SW program | Community of users | HW & SW integration | T/ Upfront p. |
| e-book reader | Add on products as service | Online store | HW & online store | T/ Upfront p. + VC |
| Emergency services | SW and duration of contract | Range of services | HW & SW integration | R/ Monthly rental |
| Electricity monitor | SW program | Pre-sale consulting | HW & SW integration | T/ Upfront p. |
| Fitness machine I | SW program | Online trainer & community | HW & SW integration | T/ Upfront p. |
| Fitness machine II | SW program | None | HW & SW integration | T/ Upfront p. |
| Gaming console | Add on products as service + SW | Online store | HW & SW integration | T/ Upfront p. + VC |
| Handheld gaming device | Add on products as service + SW | Online store | HW & SW integration | T/ Upfront p. + VC |
| Home control system | SW program | Online store | HW & SW integration | T/ Upfront p. |
| Internet table-radio | Choice of radio stations | None | HW & SW integration | T/ Upfront p. |
| Mobile phone | Add on products as service | Online store | HW & SW integration | T/ Upfront p. |
| Music player, trainer & community | Add on products as service + SW | Online store | HW & online store | T/ Upfront p. + VC |
| Music player & online store | Add on products as service + SW | Online store | HW & online store | T/ Upfront p. + VC |
| Navigation system | SW program | Online store | HW & SW integration | T/ Upfront p. |
| Personal trainer I | SW program on the net | Online trainer & community | HW & SW integration | T/ Upfront p. |

| | | | | |
|---|---|---|---|---|
| Personal trainer II | SW program | Online trainer | HW & SW integration | T/ Upfront p. |
| Personal trainer III | SW program | Online trainer & community | HW & SW integration | T/ Upfront p. |
| Physical activity monitor | SW program | Online trainer | HW & SW integration | T/ Upfront p. |
| Programmable toy | Programmable robotics | Online trainer &community | HW & SW integration | T/ Upfront p. |
| Web-based personal trainer | SW program | Online trainer | HW & SW integration | T/ Upfront p. |

Key: F–C Int. – Firm–Customer Interaction, HW – Hardware, SW – Software, R – Relationship-based, T – Transaction-based, Upfront p. – Upfront purchase, VC – Variable costs

## 4.2 Leasing & Co.

In all the cases of this cluster, individualization is only visible in the form of contract volume. As the product that is leased/rented/shared/pooled itself is standard, the individualization is done on the service component. The service component is about providing the product as a service. Hence individualization is provided on contract volume. This is done in two ways:

1. Duration of contract: the length a product is used by a customer;
2. Size of contract: the number of products a customer uses at a time.

Different kinds of marketing-integration are observed in the cases. In some cases, e.g., *luxury bag rental, DVD rental through post,* and *wedding dress rental,* marketing-integration is provided as a considerable sized collection of products is on offer (which also provides some more space for individualization). Also other kinds of marketing-integration are identified. For example, *car rental* and *car sharing* additionally also provide insurance services; *yacht sharing services* and *resort property sharing* repair and maintain the assets; and *art pieces rental services* provide logistic services. In other words, all these cases exhibit some extent of vendor consolidation, i.e. the realization of a single point of contact for a multi-component offering.

Operational-integration is present in only four of the 20 cases. In the *DVD rental through post* and *luxury bag rental* cases the suppliers have seamlessly integrated the online portal, where the customers track their wish list, with an efficient logistics system that tracks and fulfills customer wishes. *IT server services* provided effortless and seamless scalability of hardware resources. The *city bikes* provided 24/7 bike return stations spread out in a city which facilitated the return of bikes.

Firm–customer interaction depends on how often a product is used. In cases where products are occasionally used, for example, *art pieces rental services, mobile toilet services, party equipment rental, and wedding dress rental,* firm–customer interaction is transactional in nature. Logically, in such cases a pay-per-use revenue model is successfully employed. In contrast, in instances where products are regularly used, for example, *white goods, DVD rental through post, personal office space, and IT server services,* firm–customer interaction is relationship-based. In such instances the offerings employ revenue models with periodically fixed charges (see *Table 20*).

*Table 20: Data analysis – 'leasing & co.' cluster*

| Leasing & Co. | Type of individualization | Marketing-integration | Operational-integration | Firm–customer interaction |
|---|---|---|---|---|
| Art pieces rental services | Duration of contract | Collection of art pieces | None | T/ Pay per use |
| Baby prams rental | Duration of contract | Repair and maintenance | None | T/ Pay per use |
| Car rental | Duration of contract | Repair & maintenance | None | T/ Pay per use |
| Car sharing | Duration of contract | Repair & maintenance | None | R/ Monthly + VC |
| City bikes rental | Duration of contract | Repair & maintenance | 24/7 bike stations | T/ Pay per use |
| Conference room sharing | Duration and size of contract | Maintenance and operation | None | T/ Pay per use |
| Copy machines | Duration of contract | Repair & maintenance | None | R/ Monthly + VC |
| DIY tools rental | Duration of contract | Collection of DIY tools | None | T/ Pay per use |
| DVD rental through post | Size of contract | Expanding collection of DVDs | Website and logistics | R/ Monthly |
| IT server services | Size of contract | Maintenance and operation | Scalability | R/ Monthly |
| Luxury bag rental | Duration of contract | Expanding collection of bags and jewelry | Website and logistics | T/ Pay per use |

| | | | | |
|---|---|---|---|---|
| Mobile toilet services | Duration of contract | Cleaning and maintenance | None | T/ Pay per use |
| Party equipment rental | Duration of contract | Planning and executing | None | T/ Pay per use |
| Personal office space | Duration of contract | Secretary services | None | R/ Monthly + VC |
| Pet dogs rental | Duration of contract | Looking after pet dogs | None | R/ Monthly + VC |
| Resort property sharing | Duration of contract | Repair & maintenance | None | R/ Monthly + down payment |
| Trucks & moving equipment | Duration of contract | Trucks, equipment, and insurance | None | T/ Pay per use |
| Wedding dress rental | Duration of contract | Collection of wedding dresses | None | T/ Pay per use |
| White goods rental | Duration of contract | Repair & maintenance | None | R/ Monthly |
| Yacht sharing services | Duration of contract | Repair & maintenance | None | R/ Monthly + VC |

Key: F–C Int. - Firm–Customer Interaction, R - Relationship-based,
T - Transaction-based, VC - Variable costs

## 4.3 Mass Customization

As the name of the cluster suggests all the 20 cases exhibited individualization. The 'individualization of the product' is the service that is provided by supplier to the customer. Three different kinds of individualization, distinguishable from each other based on the extent of individualization taking place, are identified in the 20 cases. These are:

1. Appearance: the first type of individualization can also be characterized as cosmetic since it about individualizing the outside appearance of a product. For example, individualization in *customized golf balls* and *stationery* is about printing a unique logo on the product.
2. Fabrication: the second type involves fabrication of the product to meet the requirements of the customer. For example, individualization in *customized jeans, wedding rings*, and *wheel rims*, is about producing a product to meet the design or measurements requirements of the customer.

3. Combination: the third type of individualization is about mixing and matching base elements to meet the exact combination in the final product as required by the customer. For example, individualization in *customized breakfast cereal, dolls,* and *jam,* is about combining different standard elements to create a unique customized final product.

Marketing-integration is present in all the 20 cases, albeit limited to presale consulting (provided mostly online, in some cases through a telephone hotline). The main goal of such consulting is to clarify and simplify the customization process for the customer. It can also be viewed as a sales pitch.

Operational-integration, also present in all the cases, is provided via an online configurator which helps customers define and convey their needs to the supplier.

Firm–customer interaction in this cluster, not surprisingly, is transactional in nature. As the service is provided one time there is no requirement for a relationship-based firm–customer interaction. This is also supported by the fact that in all cases an upfront revenue model is in use (see *Table 21*).

*Table 21: Data analysis – 'mass customization' cluster*

| **Mass Customization** | **Type of individualization** | **Marketing-integration** | **Operational-integration** | **Firm–customer interaction** |
|---|---|---|---|---|
| Customized beer labels | Appearance | Pre-sale consulting | Online configurator | T/ Upfront p. |
| Customized breakfast cereal | Combination | Pre-sale consulting | Online configurator | T/ Upfront p. |
| Customized coffee | Combination | Pre-sale consulting | Online configurator | T/ Upfront p. |
| Customized dolls | Combination | Pre-sale consulting | Online configurator | T/ Upfront p. |
| Customized golf balls | Appearance | Pre-sale consulting | Online configurator | T/ Upfront p. |
| Customized handbags | Appearance | Pre-sale consulting | Online configurator | T/ Upfront p. |
| Customized jams | Combination | Pre-sale consulting | Online configurator | T/ Upfront p. |
| Customized jeans | Fabrication | Pre-sale consulting | Online configurator | T/ Upfront p. |
| Customized lamps | Appearance | Pre-sale consulting | Online configurator | T/ Upfront p. |

| | | | | |
|---|---|---|---|---|
| Customized liqueur | Combination | Pre-sale consulting | Online configurator | T/ Upfront p. |
| Customized novels | Appearance | Pre-sale consulting | Online configurator | T/ Upfront p. |
| Customized picture frames | Fabrication | Pre-sale consulting | Online configurator | T/ Upfront p. |
| Customized shoes I | Fabrication | Pre-sale consulting | Online configurator | T/ Upfront p. |
| Customized shoes II | Appearance | Pre-sale consulting | Online configurator | T/ Upfront p. |
| Customized snowboards | Appearance | Pre-sale consulting | Online configurator | T/ Upfront p. |
| Customized sofa covers | Appearance | Pre-sale consulting | Online configurator | T/ Upfront p. |
| Customized stationery | Appearance | Pre-sale consulting | Online configurator | T/ Upfront p. |
| Customized t-shirts | Appearance | Pre-sale consulting | Online configurator | T/ Upfront p. |
| Customized wedding rings | Fabrication | Pre-sale consulting | Online configurator | T/ Upfront p. |
| Customized wheel rims | Fabrication | Pre-sale consulting | Online configurator | T/ Upfront p. |

Key: F–C Int. - Firm–Customer Interaction, R - Relationship-based,
T - Transaction-based, Upfront p. - Upfront purchase

## 4.4 Solutions

In all 20 cases, individualization is about meeting the exact needs of a customer by providing the desired level of marketing-integration and operational-integration as demanded by the customer.

Marketing-integration is visible in all 20 cases. Customers benefit from consolidated vendor accountability as they can choose from a range of services that are offered by suppliers. These services consist of complementary steps found in vertical value chains that exist in different industries. They range from pre-sale consulting services, financing services, standard repair services, and maintenance services to taking over business operation for customers. For example, in the case of *communication network solutions*, the supplier took over responsibility for the running of the network. Hence the supplier, instead of being a network seller, is now a provider of network coverage as a service. Consultancy services are provided in all the cases. Many firms also provide financing services. In addition to these services, firms of course continue to provide traditional repair and maintenance contracts.

Operational-integration is also evident in all cases. In some cases it can be seen in the form of system integration. For example, in the case of *mass transport solutions*, different components from different suppliers are integrated into one seamless solution. In other cases, it can be seen in form of remote monitoring. For example, in the *aircraft engine management*, *facility management*, and *solar energy services*, remote monitoring reduces unrequired service calls, detects breakdowns before they occur and improves the total performance of assets. An integrated service offering is visible in cases where the supplier promises a final result (such as asset availability).

Firm–customer interaction in all 20 cases is relationship-based, since understanding customer needs is crucial for the success of a solution. This is also supported by the type of revenue model in use. An upfront revenue model is not used in any of the 20 cases (see *Table 22*).

*Table 22: Data analysis – 'solutions' cluster*

| **Solutions** | **Type of individualization** | **Marketing-integration** | **Operational-integration** | **Firm–customer interaction** |
|---|---|---|---|---|
| Aircraft engines | Customized level of integration | Consultancy, repair & maintenance | Remote monitoring, integrated service offerings | R/ Pay by the hour |
| Automation solutions | Customized level of integration | Engineering, consultancy, repair, maintenance & financing | Integrated service offerings | R/ Pay by the hour |
| Coffee machines | Customized level of integration | Consultancy, repair & maintenance | Integrated service offerings | R/ Monthly rental |
| Communication network solutions | Customized level of integration | Consultancy, operation & financing | System integration, remote monitoring & integrated service offering | R/ Fixed price contract |
| Crane solutions | Customized level of integration | Consultancy, repair & maintenance | Integrated service offering | R/ Monthly rental |
| Earthmoving equipment | Customized level of integration | Consultancy, repair & maintenance | Integrated service offering | R/ Monthly rental or contractual |

| | | | | |
|---|---|---|---|---|
| Elevator solutions | Customized level of integration | Consultancy, repair, maintenance & financing | Integrated service offering | R/ Monthly rental |
| Engineering machinery | Customized level of integration | Consultancy, repair & maintenance | Integrated service offerings | R/ Fixed price contract |
| Facility management | Customized level of integration | Consultancy, operation & financing | Remote monitoring | R/ Saving sharing |
| Fleet management | Customized level of integration | Consultancy, financing, repair & maintenance | Integrated service offerings | R/ Monthly rental |
| Green space management | Customized level of integration | Consultancy & operation | Integrated service offerings | R/ Monthly rental |
| Healthcare solutions | Customized level of integration | Consultancy, repair, maintenance & financing | Integrated service offerings, remote monitoring | R/ Monthly rental |
| Heating solutions | Customized level of integration | Consultancy & operation | Remote monitoring | R/ Monthly rental |
| Integrated pest management | Customized level of integration | Consultancy & operation | Remote monitoring | R/ Monthly rental |
| Laundry solutions | Customized level of integration | Consultancy, repair & maintenance | Integrated service offerings | R/ Monthly rental |
| Mass transport solutions | Customized level of integration | Consultancy, operation & financing | System integration, integrated service | R/ Fixed price contract |
| Solar energy services | Customized level of integration | Consultancy, operation & financing | Remote monitoring | R/ Monthly rental |
| Construction industry | Customized level of integration | Consultancy, operation & financing | System integration | R/ Fixed price contract |
| Tool management | Customized level of integration | Consultancy & repair & maintenance | Integrated service offerings | R/ Monthly rental |
| Warehouse trucks | Customized level of integration | Consultancy & repair & maintenance | Integrated service offerings | R/ Short to mid-term contracts |

Key: F-C Int. - Firm–Customer Interaction, R - Relationship-based,
T - Transaction-based, mgmt. - management

In the next chapter, findings based on the case analysis are presented.

# 5 Findings

Building on the analysis section it becomes evident that the four clusters of hybrid value creation vary considerably from each other. In sum, it is found that there is no standard formula for success in hybrid value creation. A cross comparison of the analyzed clusters makes it not only clear that the four value creating attributes play varying roles in different clusters, but also makes it possible to identify the key value creating attribute for each cluster.

This means that when an organization pursues hybrid value creation it should first identify its offerings with one of the four clusters of hybrid value creation. Accordingly the organization should know which value creating attribute to focus on most. For example, if an organization is active in the cluster of embedded products, it is imperative that it first focuses on the value creating attribute 'operational-integration'. Once this attribute is appropriately addressed, then the organization should also look at the remaining value attributes. *Table 23* provides an overview and compares the different value creating attributes in various clusters of hybrid value creation.

*Table 23: Overview: value creating attributes for each cluster*

| | **Type of individualization** | **Type of Marketing-integration** | **Type of Operational-integration** | **Type of Firm–customer Interaction** |
|---|---|---|---|---|
| **Embedded products** | Self-customizable SW or add on products or services | Online store/service (17); None (2); continuous monitoring services (1) | *Seamless technical-integration of HW & SW aspects* | Mainly transactional; relational (1) |
| **Leasing & Co.** | *Contract volume, i.e. size or duration of contract* | Vendor consolidation through a single point of contact | None (16); evident and geared towards increasing customer flexibility (4) | Both relational and transactional are equally seen |
| **Mass Customi-zation** | Performed on the final product | Pre-sale consulting | *Online configurator* | Purely transactional |
| **Solutions** | Providing desired extent of integration (marketing & operational) | *Consolidated vendor accountability* | Mainly about making sure that service is seamlessly integrated with the product | Purely relational |

Key: The attribute in *italic* is identified as the most crucial value creating attribute for the respective cluster.
A number in a (bracket) implies the number of offerings that meet a specific characteristic.

## 5.1 Embedded Products: Success through Operational-Integration

For the 'embedded products' cluster, operational-integration in the form of seamless technical-integration of the hardware and software aspects is found to be the main value creating attribute. It is also evident that effective individualization (passed forward to the customer) and marketing-integration in this cluster directly depend on how well the hardware and software components are integrated into one seamless offering. For example, the effectiveness of online stores (which is marketing-integration on one hand, and a gatekeeper to individualization on other), depends on how easy it is to buy and integrate new add-ons (mp3s, games, etc.) to existing equipment.

Analysis also showed that firm–customer interaction is directly related to the level of marketing-integration. If there is no marketing-integration (2 cases) or it is limited to online stores/services (17 cases) then the firm–customer interaction is transactional in nature. Only if the marketing-integration is repetitive in nature (1 case where they provided continuous monitoring services), is the firm–customer interaction (and revenue model) relational in nature. *Figure 6* shows how the four value creating attributes are related to each other. It emphasizes the importance of operational-integration for the cluster of embedded products.

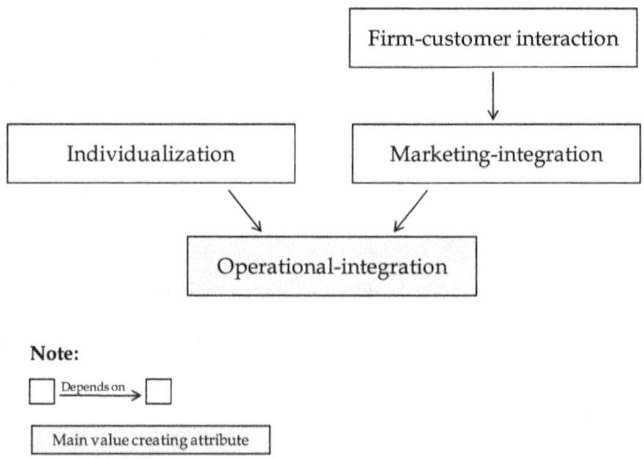


*Figure 6: Embedded Products: mapping the value creating attributes*

## 5.2 Leasing & Co.: Success through Individualization

For the 'leasing & co.' cluster, individualization in the form of contract volume (i.e. size or duration of contract) is found to be the main value creating attribute. Operational-integration, evident only in four cases, is found to have the sole aim of providing customers with increased control over how long they kept/used a product. In other words, operational-integration is geared towards increasing the possibility to individualize contracts.

Similarly, marketing-integration also focuses on increasing the possibilities to individualize by either providing the customer with a huge collection of products or complementary services to choose from. *Figure 7* shows how the four value creating attributes are related (or not related) to each other. Firm-customer interaction only depends on how often a product is used and is independent from the other value creating attributes. If an offering is used infrequently, the interaction is transactional in nature (e.g. the hiring of art pieces or mobile toilets for a specific occasion). If an offering is used regularly then the firm–customer interaction is relational in nature (e.g. white goods).

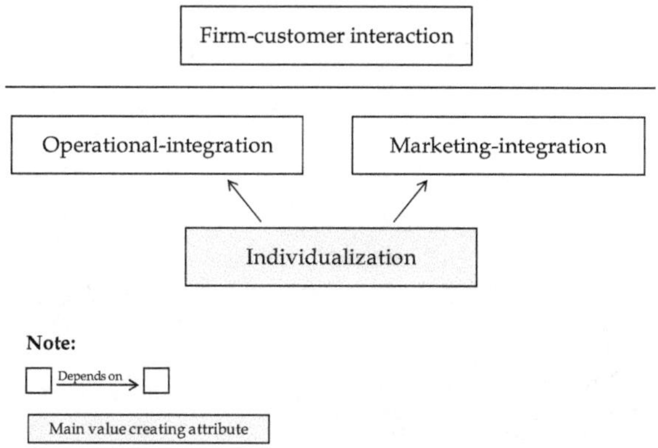


*Figure 7: Leasing & co.: mapping the value creating attributes*

## 5.3 Mass Customization: Success through Operational-Integration

The main value creating attribute in the 'mass customization' cluster is operational-integration. Even though providing an individualized product is the goal here, individualization is not identified as the main value creating attribute. This can be explained by the fact that the market success of offerings in this cluster directly depends on reaching two contradictory goals simultaneously, i.e. providing individualization without sacrificing the cost advantages of mass production.

These contradictory goals are mainly met through operational-integration in the shape of an online configurator, which plays a dual role. First, it helps customers define preferences (pre-sale consultation, i.e. marketing-integration). And second, it makes sure that customer preferences fall into a pre-defined solution space. Hence operational-integration is the essence of offerings in this cluster. *Figure 8* portrays how the value creating attributes are related (or not related) to each other. Firm–customer interaction in all 20 cases is transactional in nature. As with the leasing & co. cluster, firm–customer interaction in this cluster is independent from the other value creating attributes.

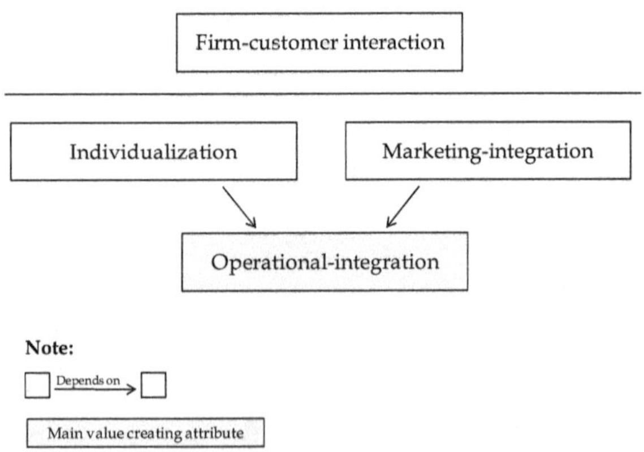


*Figure 8: Mass customization: mapping the value creating attributes*

## 5.4 Solutions: Success through Marketing-Integration

For the 'solutions' cluster, marketing-integration in the form of service offerings is found to be the main value creating attribute. The primary goal of solutions is to help customers focus on their core competencies. In other words, it is about freeing the customer from hassles that are not directly associated with their core competency. This is achieved by providing the customer with benefits of vendor consolidation (i.e. marketing-integration) as the supplier takes over a wide range of functions such as consulting, repair, and maintenance, and in some cases also the day-to-day operations.

Once a firm gets its marketing-integration in place, it should then focus on operational-integration. Operational-integration is found to be more a cost saving attribute for the supplier; especially in cases where the customer is promised a final result or outcome. Therefore, it is in the best interests of the supplier that various components interact seamlessly and increase cost saving opportunities. Also marketing-integration and operational-integration often go hand and hand and depend on each other. The intensity of firm–customer interaction, purely relational in nature, depends on the extent of the marketing-integration availed of by the customer. Individualization is directly related to the extent of marketing- and operational-integration on offer. *Figure 9* shows how the four value creating attributes are related to each other.

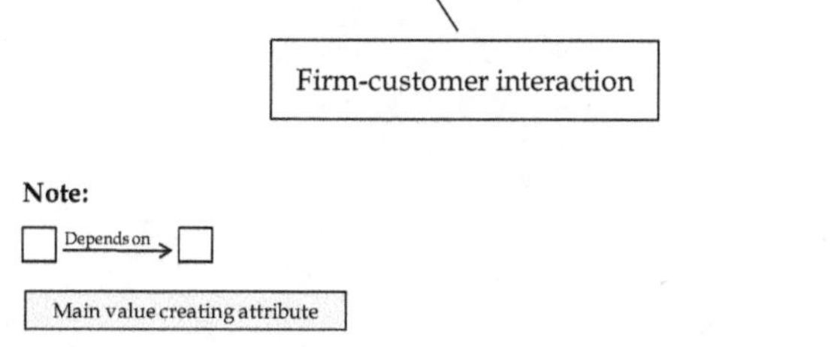


*Figure 9: Solutions: mapping the value creating attributes*

# 6 Reflection and Research Directions

This empirical study identifies four different clusters of hybrid value creation. It also finds that there is no standard formula for success in hybrid value creation. Four value creating attributes have been identified from literature and their contribution for the different clusters of hybrid value creation has been empirically derived. As a result, this study suggests a two-step strategy to increase the success of hybrid offerings. When implementing hybrid value creation:

1. First, the type of hybrid value creation has to be determined. Firms can do this by identifying to which one of the four clusters their offering belongs;
2. Second, depending on the cluster, the corresponding key value creating attribute needs to be carefully designed.

Even though all four clusters of hybrid value creation are interesting and require further research this dissertation focuses further on only two of the four clusters: *embedded products* and *solutions*. Before going deeper into the two selected clusters, the rationale for culling the other two clusters is provided. As seen from the extent of literature (provided below) dealing specifically with other two clusters - mass customization and leasing & co. - they are identified to have grown into independent research subjects and hence are no more a focus of this dissertation.

*Mass customization* has been extensively researched in the past 15+ years by many authors (Pine 1992; Pine, Victor, and Boynton 1993; Kotha 1995; Kotha 1996; Lampel and Mintzberg 1996; Hart 1996; Gilmore and Pine 1997; Broekhuizen and Alsem 2000; Duray et al. 2000; Riemer and Totz 2003; Sievänen 2004; Piller and Franke 2004; Berger et al. 2005; Blecker and Friedrich 2006; Piller 2006; Gardner 2009). With this amount of research present, mass customization has developed into an independent subject of research with an international conference (the Mass Customization and Personalization Conference) dedicated to the topic. Hence, if the reader is further interested in this cluster, she or he should focus on the vast amounts of literature present on it. The two volumes of *"Handbook of Research in Mass Customization and Personalization"* by Piller and Tseng (2010) is a good starting point to get deeper into this cluster.

For the *leasing & co.* cluster, even though this study identifies individualization as the key value creating attribute, existing research suggests that customer acceptance of such business models is the most crucial aspect for their success. Therefore, on the one hand the attractiveness and viability of leasing & co. has been extensively studied in the fields of economics, finance, and accounting (Bower, Herringer, and Williamson 1966; Gordon 1974; Lewellen, Long, and McConnell 1976; Miller and Upton 1976; Flath 1980; Ang and Peterson 1984; Grenadier 1995; Varian 2000); on the other hand research also looks at these business models from a marketing (McNeill 1944; Obenberger and Brown 1976) and consumer behavior/acceptance (Meijkamp 1998; Hirschl, Konrad, and Scholl 2003; Mont 2004b) point of view. Hence, if the reader is further interested in this cluster she or he should focus on the extant research, mentioned above, that deals with this cluster.

The focus of this dissertation is on the questions, which arise in this study, in regard to the two remaining clusters of hybrid value creation.

For the cluster of embedded products, operational-integration is identified as the main value creating attribute. Furthermore, it is noticed that two of three other value creating attributes, individualization and marketing-integration, also directly depend on the extent of operational-integration. Hence, it becomes imperative that offerings from this cluster are immaculately designed. Consequently, part IV (empirical study 2) focuses on the first step of the design process. It explores the critical aspects that should be taken into consideration when designing embedded products.

For the cluster of solutions, marketing-integration is identified as the main value creating attribute. In line with this, manufacturing firms in the recent past - by adding a host of new services to their standalone products - strive to reposition themselves as solution providers. Consequently, part V (empirical study 3) aims at better understanding this trend by building on existing theoretical contributions.

# IV

## Empirical Study 2: The Cluster of Embedded Products

# 1 The Need for Further Research on Embedded Products

Building on the findings of part III (empirical study 1), part IV further explores the cluster of embedded products[7]. The reader is reminded that embedded products are offerings where traditional or new services are embedded in the product using new digital technologies. The primary goal of embedded products is to either create:

1. A radically new offering;
2. Protect an existing product by improving the perceived use value of it.

Even though an increasing number of firms offer embedded products there is limited research and understanding on how to best combine products and services to get the most out of such offers.

In part III, operational-integration - in the form of seamless technical-integration of the hardware and software aspects - is identified as the main value creating attribute for the cluster of embedded products. *Figure 10* - presented previously in Part III - maps the value creating attributes for the cluster of embedded products.

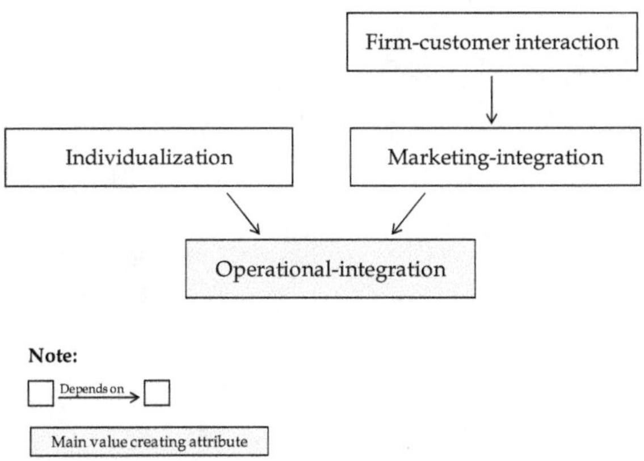


*Figure 10: Embedded products: mapping the value creating attributes*

As seen in the above figure, it is noticed that two other value creating attributes, individualization (passed forward to the customer) and marketing-integration, also

[7] Note than an earlier version of this research, with a focus on the preventive healthcare industry, was presented at the *15th International Product Development Management Conference* (IPDMC) 2008, Hamburg (see Velamuri, Neyer, and Möslein 2008). Although that publication was co-authored, the identification of relevant theory, the research design, the collection of data, the analysis of data, and the interpretation of results are primarily attributable to Vivek K. Velamuri.

directly depend on how well the hardware and software components are integrated into one seamless offering. Hence, it becomes imperative that offerings from this cluster are immaculately designed. Consequently, this study focuses on the first step of the design process in the context of embedded products. This leads to the research question:

> *What are the critical aspects that need to be taken into consideration when designing an embedded product?*

To gain a better understanding of these key aspects, six firms that offer embedded products were chosen to be interviewed. The six firms cover a broad range of embedded products: an e-book reader, a fitness machine, a gaming console, a music player, a programmable toy, and a web-based personal trainer.

The remainder of this empirical study is organized as follows. Chapter 3 identifies six critical aspects that need to be taken into consideration when designing an embedded product. Chapter 4 concludes this study by providing theoretical and practical implications and notes the limitations of this empirical study. But before that, chapter 2 describes the method used and introduces the reader to the six case studies selected for this research study.

# 2 Method and Data

This chapter introduces the reader to the research method used, the research approach undertaken and the case studies. These three aspects are contained in the following three sections.

The first section explains why the qualitative case study method is appropriate for this study. The second section - case selection - provides the criteria kept in mind when choosing the embedded products for this study. In addition, the six cases are also listed. Finally, the third section describes the research approach. This includes not only how and with whom the interviews were conducted, but also how the data was coded.

## 2.1 Research Design

The objective of this research study was to explore the cluster of embedded products to gain a better understanding of the critical aspects that need to be taken into consideration when designing an embedded product. To meet this objective, an explorative qualitative research method was chosen. More specifically, because little is known and researched in this direction, an explorative multiple case study approach was used (Yin 2003). To strengthen the resulting interferences, data from several cases were gathered and examined in an iterative way (Yin 2003). This allowed the gaining of a bigger picture of locally grounded causality (Eisenhardt 1989).

## 2.2 Case Selection

The rationale behind choosing these six case firms was to increase external validity and ensure generalization so that the findings are applicable for understanding hybrid value creation in the context of embedded products. As the firms were from different industries (which also means that they had different backgrounds, i.e. different market conditions, internal service organizations, and history), their selection follows the logic behind theoretical samplings as discussed by Eisenhardt (1989). In other words, to capture the maximum number of potential influencing factors on the design of embedded products the decision to choose the firms and embedded products was based on two aspects:

1. To have a heterogeneous setting of firms;
2. To have a heterogeneous range of embedded products.

*Table 24* lists the six embedded products chosen for this study.

*Table 24: List of six embedded products*

| **Generic name of embedded product** | **Brief description of product and service dimensions of the embedded product** |
|---|---|
| e-book reader | ▪ *Product dimension:* A miniature handheld computer which is designed for displaying e-books.<br>▪ *Service dimension:* An online shop that provides a large array of e-books, e-magazines, and e-journals to be conveniently downloaded to the e-book reader at an extra cost. |
| Fitness machine | ▪ *Product dimension:* A cycling ergo-meter with sensors that help measure the vital signs of the user.<br>▪ *Service dimension:* The software enables computer-aided recording, monitoring, and analysis of training data. 3D topographic maps build the basis for interactive training courses. |
| Gaming console | ▪ *Product dimension:* Consists of gaming console with internet connectivity, movement sensors, and controllers.<br>▪ *Service dimension:* Allows people to play against each other remotely. Various channels with news, weather, and shopping can be accessed. Many games can be purchased that can train people, for example, to cook healthily or keep fit. |
| Music player | ▪ *Product dimension:* A music player.<br>▪ *Service dimension:* An online shop provides a wide range of music and podcasts that can either be purchased or downloaded for free. |
| Programmable toy | ▪ *Product dimension:* A line of construction-toys that includes sensors, cables, and motors.<br>▪ *Service dimension:* The toys are programmable. In addition the online community allows for sharing of tricks between users of such toys. |
| Web-based personal trainer | ▪ *Product dimension:* Consists of a mobile phone, a heart-rate monitor, and a stride sensor chip that fits with regular running footwear.<br>▪ *Service dimension:* Software on the mobile phone that gives real-time feedback to the runner on his performance. The software also selects music that is most suitable to the running pattern. In addition the website allows the customization of a training program to meet the specific requirements of a customer. |

## 2.3 Research approach

Data was collected through a combination of techniques (Yin 2003). Alongside the open-ended and mostly semi-structured interviews which were the primary source of information; marketing material and web presence provided another rich source of information. All this together formed the empirical basis of this study. In total 12 product developers and/or marketing managers were interviewed. The approached managers were rather open to participate in this research study. In the end, however, the quality and not quantity of the interview partners and their willingness to disclose information were crucial for the success of this study. Fifty percent of these interviews were conducted face-to-face whereas the rest were conducted over phone. Interviews lasted 30 minutes on average.

If the interviewee agreed, the interview was taped and transcribed before data analysis. In a first step, the interviewees were asked to define an embedded product or what they understood as embedded products. In some cases they had not heard of this term. In such situations, an example of an embedded product from their product-portfolio of goods was mentioned. This made sure that the interviewees and the interviewer were talking about the same concept. In the next step, open-ended questions were asked to gain an understanding of what the interviewees see as critical aspects that influence the design of embedded products. Just before the conclusion of each interview, the interviewees were given one more opportunity to list what they thought were the most important criteria for the success of embedded products.

The text analysis followed the typical content analysis procedures to code the data (e.g. Glaser and Strauss, 1967). The coding of data into categories corresponding to the research question led to the discovery of six major categories:

1. Hybrid arrangement
2. Dimension of hybridity
3. Revenue model used
4. Web as a service platform
5. Engagement in community building
6. Integration of customer feedback.

If the data collected from the various sources was inconsistent or contradictory, then the interviewees were re-approached to clarify issues. These six dimensions are discussed in detail in the following chapter.

# 3 Findings

In this chapter, the results of the analysis and iterative comparison of the interview data is presented. In total six critical aspects that influence the design of embedded products are identified. These critical aspects either focused on strategic decisions firms need to take while designing embedded products or associated with decisions that were connected to the customer service/interaction. Consequently, they have been grouped into two categories:

1. Strategically-oriented critical aspects;
2. Service-oriented critical aspects.

Each group contains three critical aspects. They are discussed in length in the following two sections.

## 3.1 Strategically-Oriented Critical Aspects

Overall, the findings identified three strategic-oriented critical aspects. They are clustered as strategic-oriented as they deal with strategic decisions a firm has to take when providing/designing embedded products. The first critical aspect - hybrid arrangement - is connected to competencies a firm has or lacks. The second critical aspect - dimension of hybridity - deals with the embedded product itself. Finally, the third critical aspect is connected with the revenue model in use. These three critical aspects are listed and briefly explained in *Table 25*.

*Table 25: Three strategically-oriented critical aspects*

| Critical Aspect | Explanation |
|---|---|
| Hybrid arrangement | Are competencies of an external partner required for the embedded product? Does the embedded product lie within the traditional vertical value chain? |
| Dimension of hybridity | To what extent does the embedded product contain equivalent amounts of product and service? |
| Revenue model used | Is the revenue model subscription based, down payment based, or is it a combination of both? |

### 3.1.1 *Hybrid arrangement*

According to the interviews, the first critical aspect influencing the design of embedded products is defining the hybrid arrangement. This category consists of two aspects. They are:

1. If an external partner is integrated in developing/designing the embedded product;
2. If the embedded product lies in the traditional value chain of the firm.

In the study, four out of the six firms preferred to go alone rather than cooperate with another firm. This implied that they either had all the required competencies for the new embedded offering or they developed the required competencies from scratch. For instance, the firm dealing with fitness machines decided to develop the required software for its service offering on its own. As one interviewee working for the fitness equipment firm stated:[8]

> *"It is more difficult to solely distinguish on the basis of a product. It is the service component that really gives us the edge over our competition. We aim to be better in analyzing the vital signs of our users… this should be our intellectual property."*

In contrast, those firms who decided to cooperate with external partners emphasized that they consciously decided to stick to their core competencies and look for external partners as and when required. As one interviewee, working for a firm whose core business is in sports performance goods stated:

> *"We are a sports goods company and we are good at it. We don't want to develop software as we will only make a fool of ourselves."*

Such an open and clear outlook to work with external partners is also confirmed by another interviewee from the same firm who stated:

> *"… also we needed electronic hardware for our offering. We really don't have the competencies to produce or even work with such a product."*

This particular firm cooperated with three different organizations to design and roll out their embedded product. They collaborated with a technological conglomerate for the hardware aspects, a sports performance institute for designing the software-based personal trainer, and finally with a specialist in interactive online solutions to design a cutting-edge, user-friendly interactive web application which is the backbone of the service dimension.

[8] A full list of interview citations is provided in Annex B.

The second aspect checks if the embedded products are part of the traditional value chain of the firm. In the study it became evident that boundaries that governed industries had at least diluted if not completely disappeared. Having said that, one should also take into consideration the role played by information and communication technologies in destroying existing business models. An online retailer, the developer of the e-book reader, said that it would rather shape the future of its market than be forced to follow. These were views that were also shared by the fitness machine manufacturer and the music player manufacturer. In these cases, it can be stated that the embedded product - even though the embedded service was not part of the traditional definition of a vertical value chain of the firms involved - was developed by firms to protect or enhance their market position.

There is also an example of an embedded product that completely broke free from rigid industry/firm boundaries. In this particular example, a world leader in sporting goods partnered with a technology conglomerate to offer an innovative embedded product. These two firms, from two completely different industries, successfully collaborated with each other. They generated additional value by not expanding vertically in the traditional value chain, but by combining complementary products and services that lay outside the traditional vertical value chain. This finding gives impetus to a suggestion that hybrid value creation, i.e. value creation through combining products and services, could be used as an innovation strategy to create new offerings that create a new market (Möslein and Kölling 2007).

### 3.1.2 *Dimension of hybridity*

The second critical aspect identified in the interviews is the dimension of hybridity. This describes whether firms give equal importance to both the product and service dimension of their embedded products. Literature states that for hybrid value creation, a customer requirement is fulfilled through an optimal combination of products and services (Manzini and Vezzoli 2002; Tukker 2004; Möslein and Kölling 2007; Möslein and Velamuri 2009).

Two out of the six firms - those producing the music player and e-book reader - saw the product as the gateway to repetitive revenues. In both the cases the product is geared towards facilitating the use of their respective service offers (in the form of online shops selling mp3s and e-books). As a manager from one of these firms stated:

> *"The e-book reader is a gateway to future revenues. Books on demand anytime and everywhere! This is how business will be."*

Another interviewee stated:

> *"... once people get comfortable with this technology they will really start appreciating the advantages of on-demand music. Instant delivery! No CD! No scratches! No space required to store your collection. And your whole collection is mobile."*

It is also evident that the success of both these embedded products is dependent on how well the product and the online shop were technically integrated. One interviewee added that:

> *"Convenience is the key to success. It has to be very easy and simple to use the online shop in connection with the product."*

In contrast, the managers from other firms did not opine that the two dimensions - product and service - combined together to fulfill the specific needs of a customer. They mostly describe the service dimension of their embedded product as an add-on. For instance, the firm producing fitness equipment decided to offer sophisticated software (for creating individualized trainings plans) as an add-on. Despite the fact that the firm believed that software was adding a lot of value and is a crucial component of their offering, it was not willing to charge its customers for the added service dimension. In sum, the firm was now selling a product with some extra service attached.

Even though the interviewees emphasized that their offering was a genuine embedded product, it was evident that the service aspect was not taken seriously and/or they did not believe that it would be possible to monetize it successfully. As one interviewee stated:

> *"... the service aspect is not elaborate enough. It is only an add-on to our core product."*

Further discussion with these managers led to the conclusion that firms often lacked knowledge about how to exploit and monetize the service component of the embedded products. This is also reflected in the next critical aspect identified, namely the revenue model used.

### 3.1.3 *Revenue model used*

Building on previous research on embedded products, the interviews were analyzed to check whether the *revenue model used* is identified as a critical aspect that might influence the design of embedded products. In order to design successful product-service combinations, the emphasis should shift from a single transaction to a more long-term relationship with the customer (Windahl and Lakemond 2006). This should also be reflected in the revenue model used (Rocchi 2005). Consequently, one can argue that the applied revenue model can be used as a proxy to better understand the importance given to the embedded product.

Thus, the data were screened to identify what type of revenue models are used in conjunction with embedded products. Building on the findings of Windahl and Lakemond (2006), when a down payment model is used - i.e. one financial transaction between the seller and the buyer - it can be assumed that firms treat their embedded product as any other traditional product. In particular, this means that firms don't know how to monetize the service dimension as a valuable element of the embedded product. However, if a subscription-based model is used - i.e. financial transactions are made on a periodical basis to use the product - it can be argued that firms are interested in a long-term relationship with their customers, thus engaging in embedded products.

Interestingly, the data reveals that none of the embedded products used a subscription-based revenue model. Three out of the six firms used a single financial transaction model. As one manager working for the firm producing fitness machines stated:

> *"We have never used a subscription revenue model. Hence it is something we are not used to."*

This can explain to a certain degree why this firm is not monetizing the service aspect of their offering. Similarly another manager from the firm that claims to produce total fitness solutions stated:

> *"... subscription is for newspapers and magazines, and it does not suit our business. This is too radical for our taste."*

The same manager later also stated that:

> *"I can't ask my customer to buy an expensive gadget and then ask him to pay extra every month."*

The remaining firms, in addition to the single transaction, where they sold the main product, hoped to generate further revenue from the sale of add-on products. These were in the form of e-books, music or games. Here again, the firms focused on monetizing the product dimension, but not the service dimension. As one manager said:

*"... a real service would be when music is not purchased. But customers pay a monthly fee to have access to all the music that is available."*

## 3.2 Service-Oriented Critical Aspects

In addition to the strategic-oriented critical aspects discussed previously, three service-oriented critical aspects were also identified. The first critical aspect deals with the use of web as service platform. The second critical aspect deals with the engagement in community building. Finally, the third is related to the integration of customer feedback into the design/development process. These three critical aspects are listed and briefly explained in *Table 26*.

*Table 26: Three service-oriented critical aspects*

| Critical Aspect | Explanation |
|---|---|
| Web as a service platform | Is the web used as a platform to provide services? |
| Engagement in community building | Were there any community building steps taken by the embedded product provider? |
| Integration of customer feedback | Is the firm actively looking to integrate customer feedback into the design/development process? |

### 3.2.1 *Web as a service platform*

The findings show that all the firms are using the web as a service platform to reach their customers, but they had different ways of taking advantage of the internet. For example, the e-book reader and the music player were complemented with an online store (other offers also had online stores, but only in these two cases was the online store the main service aspect of the offering). As one interviewee stated:

*"The success of our strategy is directly dependent on how well our online shop is integrated in the whole offer."*

This was also reiterated by another interviewee who said:

*"The goal of making more revenues through selling more e-books directly depends on how the customers perceive our service offering in the form of the online store."*

In the case of the web-based personal trainer the main service component, the personal-trainer program, was provided over the web. Users could log on to the online system and create customized plans to meet their requirements. It was the most advanced interactive training system as it collected and used personal data to create individual training plans based on one's fitness level and specific goals. After each workout, users could upload their statistics to the online system. This helped the firm gain rich data on how the customers were using their embedded product. As one interview responsible for this embedded product stated:

> *"We could have provided the same trainer as an offline tool. But it was a very good decision to go for an ASP (application service provider) based solution. Now with so much information we are in a position to really understand our customers."*

In contrast, the firm providing the fitness machine was currently providing an offline tool (that can be downloaded on the web). However, the firm also planned to introduce its trainer on an ASP basis in the near future. In addition to the online stores, cases also exhibited other web-based services including online helpdesks, tips, instruction manuals, and communities. Engagement in online communities was given special importance by many of the interviewees. Hence it has been considered a separate critical aspect and it is discussed independently below.

### 3.2.2 *Engagement in community building*

The findings show that four out of six firms are engaging in community building to some extent. The e-book reader was one of the two cases which currently did not engage in community building. But the firm was contemplating building a community where users could share reviews on books and find others with similar reading tastes. A reading group (a book club) that spread across national boundaries was the ultimate goal. As one manager working for this firm stated:

> *"We do see the benefits of building a community. We have been successful in building a film community and we want to replicate this. But it will be open to all people who read books. Not just e-books."*

The firm with the fitness machine also had no online community on offer. The firm did realize the potential of online communities, but was inhibited in building one as it lacked the competencies. An employee working for the firm stated:

> *"We are an engineering firm. Not an internet startup. But we know we want to build a community. All our competitors are building one. But it is not easy for us."*

The other firms were actively building online communities for their customers to share their experiences with their peers and the firm. The main benefit these firms noticed was that this made the product interactive. An interviewee working for the toy firm stated:

> *"Our customers are unique. Playing with programmable toys as a hobby is not for everyone. So our community is an integral part of the offer as it brings together scattered users from all over the globe into contact with each other. They share, they juggle ideas. It adds tremendous value to our offering."*

Similarly, the firm providing the web-based personal trainer had identified the potential of community building. The community was developed as a core service aspect of the whole offering. The online sport community alone played an important role in motivating people to do more sport. Users could measure, compare, and compete with each other in a friendly environment.

### 3.2.3 *Integration of customer feedback*

Windahl et al. (2004) emphasize the need for customer interaction for the successful implementation of product–service combinations. They state that product-focused firms moving towards supplying product–service combinations need to orient themselves towards the interaction co-production mode (Windahl et al. 2004). This is in line with open innovation literature showing the crucial role of the customer in the innovation process (e.g. Hippel 1986; Piller and Walcher 2006). Thus, if firms want to innovate, they should seriously look at integrating customers into the development process of embedded products.

The data showed that all the six firms considered customer feedback to be crucial and an important source of innovation. Saying this, it is interesting to note that only three firms were actively seeking to gather customer feedback for their embedded products. One of these firms, producing web-based personal trainers, was in the process of integrating customer feedback. An interviewee from this firm stated:

> *"We are in discussion to open a call-center to cater to the specific needs of our embedded product users. We also want to inform ourselves how the customers use our embedded product. And what their expectations are."*

Interestingly, a few interviewees, coming from firms that did not actively integrate customers, suggested that cultural inertia (of the firms concerned) was to blame for not actively integrating customers. Even though the firm's product portfolio had expanded to include embedded products, instead of looking at customers as a source of innovation these firms were dead against integrating them into the development process. For instance, the marketing manager working for the firm producing fitness machines said,

> *"... we use a marketing push strategy. The techies design and produce our products. They have no contact with our customers and limited contact with us."*

The marketing manager from another firm that was not integrating customers into the development process stated:

> *"... I am told what to sell. I am the one who comes in direct contact with customer. But I never have the chance to get in touch with the technical department. To be honest, I don't think they are really interested."*

Such firms were found to be technology driven and not customer driven. This led to dysfunctional firm behavior as stated above.

In this chapter, the six critical aspects that need to be taken into consideration when designing embedded products have been discussed. Based on these finding, the next chapter portrays theoretical and practical implications for the design of embedded products.

# 4 Reflection

In general, this empirical study explores embedded products, a cluster of hybrid value creation business models, to contribute to an ongoing discussion on best practices for combining products and services. Specifically, this study focuses on the first step of the design process in the context of embedded products. It identifies six critical aspects that should be taken into consideration when designing embedded products. The findings of this study have both theoretical and practical implications for the systematic design of embedded products.

The findings offer first insights into how firms are designing (or not) embedded products in the way they do it. Results show that both the strategically- and service-oriented components that influence the design of embedded products offer a possible explanation why the service aspects of embedded products are not monetized. The findings also lead to the conclusion that firms need to align the strategic and the service component of their embedded products. This approach to designing embedded products from both a strategic and service component point of view supports previous research emphasizing the need to look at embedded products as an innovation strategy to create new markets and new lines of products (Möslein and Kölling 2007). This change in perspective required to design successful embedded products is often not practiced.

On a related note, the findings propose that firms have to become aware that offering embedded products is more than just the bundling of products and services that are part of a traditional value chain. As shown in the cases, there are firms that have been successful in offering embedded products by combining products and services that rest outside a traditional value chain. Hence, this study contradicts previous research conducted by Wise and Baumgartner (1999), who suggest that embedded products only combine products and services that belong to a traditional vertical value chain.

Third, the findings support previous research conducted (e.g. Windahl et al. 2004) by suggesting that customers should play a central role in designing embedded products. Even though a lot of research has been conducted to understand the role of the customer in the innovation process (e.g. von Hippel 1986; Chesbrough 2003; Baldwin, Hienerth, and von Hippel 2006; Füller et al. 2006; Hienerth 2006; Lettl, Herstatt, and Gemuenden 2006; Prügl and Schreier 2006; Reichwald and Piller 2009);

this area has received limited attention, by both research and practice, in the context of embedded products.

However, the findings show that all interviewed managers acknowledge the advantages of integrating customers in the process of designing embedded products. Hence, future research should aim to study how different tools and strategies known from the open innovation literature, such as lead user method (von Hippel 1986; Lüthje and Herstatt 2004) or idea contests (Piller and Walcher 2006), can be applied in the context of embedded products.

The findings derive four important practical implications. The first lesson learned is that firms need to go beyond their applied 'trial-and-error strategy' when designing embedded products. It is not about just combining products and services; it is about understanding what products and services should be combined and in what manner so that a firms comes up with a seamless offering. Closely related to this is the second lesson learned: that for the successful design of embedded products, managers need to think about the embedded product not as a bundling strategy but as an innovation strategy. Firms need to think about the interconnection between the strategic and service aspects when designing embedded products. For example, a revenue model needs to be designed in such a way that it supports the acceptance of service components such as community building in the context of the whole offer. By not taking such an approach while designing an embedded product, firms are primed to fail with their offerings in the market. The third lesson learned is that firms need to think outside the box to come up with novel embedded products. This means that firms need to look outside the traditional value chain to identify products and services to combine. By doing this in a systematic and strategic manner, firms could be able to design radically new embedded products and thus create new markets. The final lesson learnt is that firms need to integrate customers in the design process. As mentioned previously this is also identified as a direction for future research.

The strengths of this study must be tempered with recognition of its limitations. The interviewee sample was relatively small, which is a common trade-off in qualitative research. A related limitation is that the sample, consisting of six case firms, does not offer an exhaustive variety of organizations or embedded products. The method used was appropriate, since the aim was to capture depth of understanding in this specific study, rather than breadth at this explorative phase. In qualitative case study research, one cannot generalize from the selected sample to the whole population. Hence, of course the findings may not applicable for designing all embedded products. But this does not negate the quality of results that firms need to align the strategic and the service component of their embedded products.

In conclusion, this empirical study contributes to a better understanding of the critical aspects that influence the design of embedded products. Empirical evidence on how strategic-oriented as well as service-oriented aspects may influence the design of embedded products has so far been limited. This research sheds some light on this relation, and thus can help both firms and researchers that want to better understand and design embedded products. Overall, the findings show that firms do not really know how to integrate the service dimension to use it as a driver for value creation. Nevertheless, all firms exhibited the urge to improve their service dimension.

# V

# Empirical Study 3: The Cluster of Solutions

# 1 The Need for Further Research on Solutions

Building on the findings of part III (empirical study 1), this part further explores the 'solutions' cluster[9]. The reader is reminded that solutions are defined as seamless offerings of products and services that meet customer's individual needs. The primary goal of a solution-based business model is to help customers focus on their core competencies.

In part III, marketing-integration in the form of vendor consolidation is identified as the main value creating attribute for the cluster of solutions. *Figure 11* - presented previously in part III - maps the value creating attributes for the 'solutions' cluster.

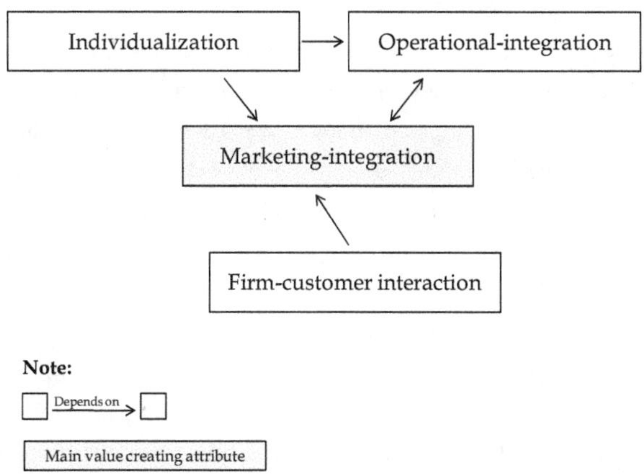


*Figure 11: Solution: mapping the value creating attributes*

As seen in the above figure, it is noticed that individualization, operational-integration and firm–customer interaction are directly connected to marketing-integration. Marketing-integration is about freeing the customer from hassles not directly associated with their core competency. Vendor consolidation is provided to the customer by providing a wide range of service functions such as business

[9] Note that a refined version of this research been accepted for publication in the *International Journal of Innovation Management* (see Velamuri et al. 2013). Although that publication was co-authored, the identification of relevant theory, the research design, the collection of data, the analysis of data, and the interpretation of results are primarily attributable to Vivek K. Velamuri.

consulting, financing, repair, maintenance, and in some cases support in day-to-day operations. Hence, this study explores the 'solutions' cluster to better understand the dynamics of marketing-integration provided by firms.

In the last decade, competition in the manufacturing industry has become more intense and price aggressive. Incumbent industry players are constantly confronted by the reality that product-based differentiation is extremely difficult and more expensive to preserve than ever before. The rapid development of information and communication technology (ICT) and the liberalization of international trade have also played a crucial role in broadening the access to alternatives for the customer (Quinn, Doorley, and Paquette 1990; Sharma and Molloy 1999; Teece 2009). Wu et al. (2006) suggest that firms which manufacture in the US need to cut their prices by at least 30% or risk losing out to Chinese competition. They also state that this rule holds good for not only low-technology goods such as apparel, but also high-technology goods such as telecommunication equipment. All this, in no way detrimental to overall economic progress, is pushing manufacturing firms to look for new sources of competitive advantage. In particular, manufacturing firms are re-evaluating their business models to improve the value proposition they offer to their customer (Teece 2009). In other words, firms are looking to conduct business in fundamentally different manner than before, i.e. to engage in "strategic innovation"[10] (Markides 1997).

Management scholars suggest that strategic innovation is a crucial variable in providing superior customer value and achieving competitive advantage (Chesbrough 2007). It is about challenging the existing taken-for-granted way of doing business (Hamel 1998; Markides 1997; Christensen, Johnson, and Rigby 2002; Tucker 2001; Kim and Mauborgne 1997). Kim and Mauborgne (1997; 1999; 2005) state that strategic innovation is achieved when a firm's actions simultaneously drive up value for buyers (customers) and drive down costs for sellers (suppliers). Strategic innovation is more than just innovation as it requires firms to achieve a leap in value for both themselves and their customers.

Not surprisingly, manufacturing firms especially from the advanced economies are seeking to engage in strategic innovation by providing a host of downstream services valued by customers (Oliva and Kallenberg 2003). By going downstream and providing complementary services, firms are providing marketing-integration to their customers. In other words, customers are able to acquire different

[10] Beware of phraseology. Different terms such as "strategy innovation", "value innovation" and "disruptive innovation" have been used to describe similar phenomena that are subsumed under the term "strategic innovation".

components from a single supplier. On the other hand, firms to their advantage are able to generate additional revenues and differentiate themselves from their low cost competitors (Gebauer, Fleisch, and Friedli 2005). In the process, manufacturing firms are repositioning themselves from sellers of products to solvers of customer problems. They are calling themselves solution providers (Sharma and Molloy 1999).

Research has also identified that firms have not been financially successful with a move downstream into services. Even though this has led to an increase in overall sales (turnover), the profitability as a percentage of sales is actually decreasing (Neely 2008). Hence this study looks at solutions from a strategic innovation perspective and explains how firms can go about achieving profitability with solutions. This leads us to the research question:

> *What should be the logic behind a firm's strategy to implement a solution-based business model?*

So far, existing research on the solution-based business models is mainly available in the context of complex product systems (abbreviated as CoPS) that are high cost, technology-intensive constructs (e.g. telecommunication networks) (Davies and Brady 2000; Rush, Michael Hobday, and Tidd 2000; Hardstone 2004; Flowers 2004; Prencipe 1998; Paoli and Prencipe 1999; Hansen and Rush 1998). These are normally one off projects where the emphasis is on design, project management, system engineering, and system integration.

In contrast, this study focuses on solution-based business models in the context of firms that produce standardized capital goods in large volumes. It builds on existing theoretical contributions by drawing from case study research undertaken with four international manufacturing firms operating in different industries: laundry (Electrolux), healthcare (Siemens), climate control (Viessmann), and cleaning (Wetrok) to meet two main goals:

1. To analyze how such firms aim to improve the value proposition they offer to their customer. Here five distinct services are identified that support extant solution-based business model literature.
2. To demonstrate that firms through solution-based business models aim at strategic innovation. For this, the innovation framework of Kim and Mauborgne (2005) is used.

The remainder of this empirical study is organized as follows. Chapter 2 provides the theoretical underpinning of solution-based business models. Chapter 3 contains the case studies and describes the research method and approach used. Chapter 4 identifies new service offerings provided by the firms. In addition, it also demonstrates that firms aim at strategic innovation through solution-based business models. Chapter 5 concludes this study by noting the limitation and drawing theoretical and practical implications.

# 2 Theoretical Underpinning

Value has consistently migrated downstream from manufacturing to services in the past two decades (Goldman, Nagel, and Preiss 1994; Wise and Baumgartner 1999; Auramo and Ala-Risku 2005; Ala-Risku 2007; Velamuri, Neyer, and Möslein 2008). In line with this, references can be found in literature from manufacturing, strategy, and marketing disciplines. Literature from the manufacturing discipline proposes that firms should integrate services into their product offerings and move to service the installed base (e.g. Oliva and Kallenberg 2003; Azarenko et al. 2009). Literature from strategy advocates capturing a larger chunk of the value chain (e.g. Gadiesh and Gilbert 1998; Potts 1988). Service-dominant logic has continued this discussion on both a theoretical level (Vargo and Lusch 2004; 2006) and on a practical level (Neu and Brown 2005; Sawhney 2006) in the marketing discipline. This chapter looks at the motivation for and viability of providing solutions. Finally, it looks at the evolution of research on service classifications and business models in the context of solutions.

## 2.1 Motivation and Viability

Securing profits is the ultimate force behind manufacturing firms' moving into the new paradigm of hybrid value creation, i.e. moving away from being a pure product seller to selling combinations of products and services. For a profitable transition, two crucial conditions need to be met. First, a firm needs to be motivated to provide services (compulsion is *negative motivation*). And second, providing services needs to be viable, i.e. make financial sense (be profitable), as motivation alone does not suffice for a successful foray into services. These two conditions are briefly examined below.

### *2.1.1 Motivation*

In general, services promise higher returns due to the shrinking margins for manufactured goods (Anderson, Fornell, and Rust 1997). Revenue streams from services are less likely to be adversely affected by downturns in the economy when compared to revenue streams generated from the sale of capital goods (Brady, Davies, and Gann 2005b). Firms are also motivated by the fact that they can gain a competitive advantage by offering integrated product-service combinations (Mont

2004a). On the one hand, firms can move up the value chain (Zaring et al. 2001) and on the other hand, such combinations are more difficult to imitate, as the service aspect is less tangible. This leads to a competitive advantage that is easier to sustain (Heskett, Sasser, and Schlesinger 1997). In addition, customers demand such solutions as they pay more attention to life cycle costs than before (Hartmann and Girmscheid 2004). Firms are also increasingly concentrating on their core competencies and outsourcing many functions in search of saving costs (Oliva and Kallenberg 2003).

### 2.1.2 *Viability*

Being profitable while providing services is the second requirement. Firms have two generic strategies to choose from: low cost or differentiation (Porter 1998). They can either provide services cheaper than the competition (cost based) or provide superior services at a price premium (differentiation based).

In the context of solutions, a cost-based strategy could be based on the fact that manufacturing firms may have extensive implicit knowledge of their products (Harrison 2004; Bennett, Sharma, and Tipping 2001). They could exploit this knowhow to compete on a cost basis (for instance by eliminating unrequired service calls). A differentiation strategy could be based on the value creating attributes previously described in part III. These are:

1. *Individualization:* the offering is individualized to meet specific customer needs better than other existing options;
2. *Marketing-Integration:* the offering provides the benefits of vendor consolidation;
3. *Operational-Integration*: the offering seamlessly integrates the various components such that it helps the customer in avoiding extra effort, time and risk;
4. *Firm–customer interaction:* the customer perceives the purchasing process as a desirable and positive experience.

## 2.2 Evolution of Service Classifications and Solution-based Business Models

Even though Levitt was the first to hint towards the solution business when he introduced the total product concept (Levitt 1980), Vandermerwe and Rada (1988) were the first to delve deeper into the concept. They stated that fuller offering consisted of a customer-focused combination of goods, services, support, self-service, and knowledge. Since then, extant research has focused on classifying services and solution-based business models. These are presented below.

The reader is reminded not to confuse the business models classification (four clusters of hybrid value creation) proposed in part III with the business models presented in this chapter. In part III, the four clusters of business models developed were a generic classification for all product-service combinations. Whereas the solution-based business model classifications presented in this chapter solely focus on the solutions cluster.

### *2.2.1 Evolution of service classifications*

Initially, research focused on classifying the service aspects of combined offerings. Kotler suggested that industrial services[11] should be classified into either *maintenance and repair services* or *business advisory services* (Kotler 1994). While some researchers suggested that it was more useful to classify product services into either *transaction related services* or *relationship related* services (Frambach, Wels-Lips, and Gündlach 1997), others insisted that the classification of industrial services should be based on the point-in-time of delivery and came up with three categories: *pre-purchase services, services delivered at purchase,* and *after-sales services* (Homburg and Garbe 1999). Another classification proposed, based on the intended target of the delivered service, distinguishes between *services supporting the product (SSP)* and *services supporting the client (SSC)* (Mathieu 2001b). This is an extension of the classification scheme proposed by Kotler (1994).

Using firm–customer interaction (transactional or relational) as one dimension and orientation of service (product or customer's process) as the second dimension, Oliva and Kallenberg (2003) provided a 2*2 matrix with four identified service categories: *basic installed services, maintenance services, operational services,* and *professional services.* A classification with similar categories is suggested by Brady, Davies, and Gann (2005a), who state that the four service categories - *system integration services, operational services, business consulting,* and *financing services* - are provided during different life cycle stages of a solution offering. *Table 27* provides an overview of various service classifications.

[11] Beware of phraseology. Some authors distinguish between industrial services and product services. For this study no such distinction has been made between them.

*Table 27: Various service classifications*

| Year | Author(s) | Logic | Classification |
|---|---|---|---|
| 1994 | Kotler | Service orientation (intended target of the services) | ▪ maintenance and repair services<br>▪ business advisory services |
| 1997 | Frambach, Wels-Lips, and Gündlach | Firm–customer interaction | ▪ transaction based<br>▪ relationship based |
| 1999 | Homburg and Garbe | Point-in-time of delivery | ▪ pre-purchase services<br>▪ services delivered at purchase<br>▪ after-sales services |
| 2001 | Mathieu | Service orientation (intended target of the services) | ▪ services supporting product (SSP)<br>▪ services supporting the client (SSC) |
| 2003 | Oliva and Kallenberg | 2*2 matrix; the 2 axes are firm–customer interaction intensity (see above in table) and intended target of the services (see above in table) | ▪ basic installed services<br>▪ maintenance services<br>▪ operational services<br>▪ professional services |
| 2005a | Brady, Davies, and Gann | Life cycle stages | ▪ system integration services<br>▪ operational services<br>▪ business consulting services<br>▪ financing services |

### *2.2.2 Evolution of solution-based business models*

Competitive advantage is not derived by just adding services to products, but it is derived how the products and services are combined with each other. Hence, one must look at what has been researched and proposed in the context of solution-based business models.

Sharma and Molloy (1999) state that a solution-based business model should help the customer in either: (1) *improving their operating performance*, (2) *increasing their asset effectiveness*, (3) *expanding their market*, and (4) *mitigating risks (price, volume, technology)*. Wise and Baumgartner (1999) identify four downstream business models for moving into services: (1) *embedded services*, (2) *comprehensive services*, (3) *integrated solutions*, and (4) *distribution control*. *Embedded services* are downstream services (e. g. fault reporting) that are built into the hardware (embedded) using digital technologies. *Comprehensive services* include services that range from financing the sale to the customer to helping the customer in maintaining and operating his business. *Integrated solutions* are seamless offerings of products and services that are a complete answer - including risk mitigation - to a given customer problem. These three downstream business models are consistent with at least one of the four objectives identified by Sharma and Molloy (1999). For example, embedded services help customers in not only improving their operating performance, but also in increasing their asset effectiveness. *Table 28* provides an overview of what objectives are met by each of these downstream business models. The fourth downstream business model, *distribution control*, has not been considered as it suggests expanding to a new position in the value chain at the cost of the customer.

*Table 28: Downstream business models and objectives met*

| **Downstream business models** (Wise and Baumgartner 1999) | **Four broad objectives** (Sharma and Molloy 1999) Help customers in: |
|---|---|
| Embedded services | ✓ improving their operating performance<br>✓ increasing their asset effectiveness |
| Comprehensive services | ✓ improving their operating performance<br>✓ increasing their asset effectiveness<br>– mitigating risk<br>– expanding their market |
| Integrated solutions | ✓ improving their operating performance<br>✓ increasing their asset effectiveness<br>✓ mitigating risk<br>✓ expanding their market |

✓ Primary objective
– Also achieved to some extent

Allmendinger and Lombreglia (2005) suggest that a solution-based business model should revolve around the life cycle of a product. The product, so to say, is the gateway to a large variety of high-value services that should be built around the product. Harrison (2003) proposes three ways to go beyond the product and states that any new service on offer should be based on the intellectual property of a firm. He suggests that a firm could choose from being:

1. an *educational provider* (provide trainings and customize educational materials to suit customer requirements);
2. a *diagnostic provider* (alleviate customer problems - those the customer can't solve internally - through providing additional services); and
3. a *discovery provider* (analyze and improve the business processes of the customer).

Roy elaborates four financially and environmentally sustainable service strategies: (1) *result oriented services* where an agreed-upon result is delivered, (2) *shared utilization services* where asset utilization is improved, (3) *product-life extension services* where product lifespan is extended, and (4) *demand side management* where integrated source management helps reduce wastages (Roy 2000).

In sum, research presents different classification models for services and suggests that solution-based business models should help customers achieve better outcomes. The studies, however, have only divulged options for going downstream, but have not explained how firms can be financially successful when venturing downstream. As previously mentioned, research has stated that firms moving downstream into solutions have reduced profitability as percentage of total sales (Neely 2008). Hence, this study looks at solutions from a strategic innovation perspective and explains how firms should go about achieving profitability when delivering solutions.

# 3 Method and Data

This chapter introduces the reader to the research method used, the research approach undertaken and the case studies. These three aspects are contained in three different sections.

The first section explains why the qualitative case study method is used. The second section describes the research approach. This includes how the data was collected and analyzed. Finally, the third section deals with the data. Here the rationale behind choosing the four firms is provided. In addition the four case studies are presented in the form of vignettes.

## 3.1 Research Design

Because this research study examines the solutions cluster to understand an ongoing (contemporary) challenge of how firms should go about achieving profitability (in a real-life context) when delivering solutions, the case study method stands out as the most appropriate path to achieve it. Also case studies allow for flexibility - especially when combined with open-ended questions - that is required for explorative research and theory building. In line with this, an explorative multiple case study approach was applied (Yin 2003). The cross-comparison between the four cases strengthened the resulting interferences resulting in the creation of new variables and relationships and aimed at the exploration of theoretical explanations for the phenomenon under study (Eisenhardt 1989).

## 3.2 Research Approach

Data was collected through a combination of techniques (Yin 2003). Alongside the open-ended and mostly semi-structured interviews which were the primary source of information, the marketing materials, web presences, and customer service hotlines provided a rich source of information that formed the empirical basis of this study. Multiple interviews with at least two managers working in sales and/or service and/or the commercial departments[12] of the selected firms were conducted. The rather high willingness of managers to participate in this study was pleasantly

---

[12] One must note that many managers worked for hybrid departments, i.e., their responsibilities crossed over traditional departmental boundaries.

surprising. In the end, however, the quality and not quantity of the interview partners and their willingness to disclose information were crucial for the success of this research project. Interviews lasted an hour on average. If the interviewee agreed, the interview was taped and transcribed before data analysis. In a first step, the concept of solution-based business models is clarified to the interviewees. This is to make sure that the interviewees and the interviewer were talking about the same concept. In a next step, open-ended questions were asked to gain an understanding of the desired. The interviews were concluded by giving the interviewees a final opportunity to state whatever they thought would enrich the case studies and facilitate reaching the research goals. If the data collected from various sources was inconsistent, the interview partners were re-approached to clarify issues. This was done on four occasions.

## 3.3 Case Studies

The rationale behind choosing the four firms under study was to increase external validity and ensure generalization so that the findings are applicable for understanding solution-based business models in the context of firms that produce standardized capital goods in large volumes. As the firms were from four different industries (which also means that they have different backgrounds, i.e. different market conditions, internal service organizations, and history), their selection follows the logic behind the theoretical samplings discussed by Eisenhardt (1989). The case studies of the four firms selected are presented below. In addition, mind maps showcasing the service portfolio for each case have also been presented. These mind maps were constructed from information gathered from interviews and secondary data.

### 3.3.1 *Electrolux – World leader in laundry systems*

Electrolux, a leading supplier of professional laundry systems worldwide, is part of an appliance group that is one of the world's top five home and professional appliance manufacturers. The firm, which has been in the laundry business for over 100 years, offers a comprehensive range of laundry products including washers, tumble dryers, ironers, feeders, folders, stackers, finishing equipment, and auxiliaries. The typical clients of Electrolux are individual businesses – everything from the laundries of hotels, hospitals, and apartment houses to commercial laundry operations and coin-operated launderettes. Essentially the firm targets all large-scale laundry operations.

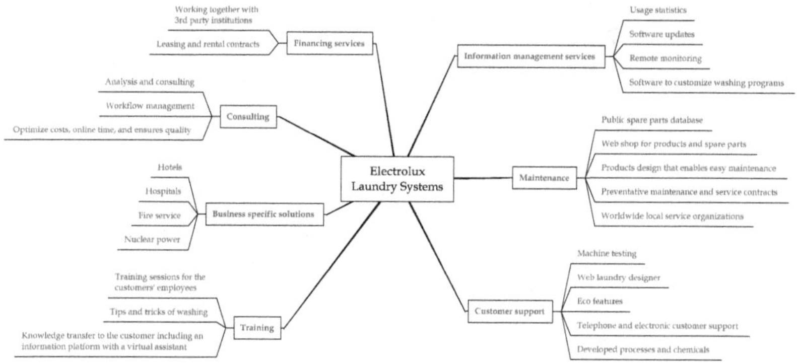


*Figure 12:* ***Mind map: Electrolux laundry systems***

The firm has operations in over 80 countries in all corners of the world. Electrolux is renowned for its innovative approach to product development, laundry processes, and production engineering worldwide. The firm has built an extensive service network over the years and perceives it as a competitive advantage. In the past few years the firm has built business-specific solutions with both product and service components to provide customized solutions. In addition, the firm is moving into educational services, managing usage information (machine statistics) to reduce downtimes, and providing financing options (see *Figure 12* for an overview of the services provided by Electrolux Laundry Systems).

### 3.3.2 *Siemens – World leader in healthcare systems*

Siemens healthcare systems, a unit of the diversified engineering conglomerate Siemens, is a global leader in the healthcare industry. The firm, which has been in the healthcare business for over 100 years, offers a wide range of medical equipment to diagnose, contain, and treat diseases. Its product range today includes imaging systems (x-ray, radiography, ultrasound, etc.), patient monitoring systems, radiation therapy equipment, respiratory machines, and hearing aids.

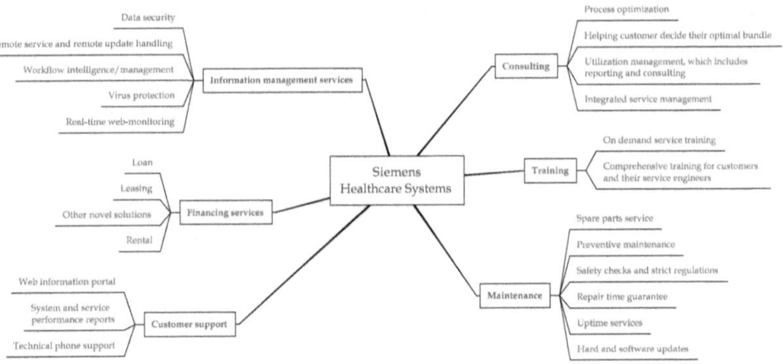


*Figure 13: Mind Map: Siemens healthcare systems*

The firm has operations in over 100 countries. Typical clients are public and private hospitals except for small consumer products, such as hearing instruments, which are directly marketed to the end consumer. The healthcare industry in the industrialized world is undergoing a radical transformation in how it functions with a focus on increasing efficiency. Siemens healthcare systems unit is at the forefront of this change. Instead of being a traditional product seller, the firm is bringing together innovative medical technologies, information systems, management consulting, and a wide range of support services to create customer-oriented solutions. The firm aims to improve efficiency in healthcare through optimizing medical processes and reducing equipment downtimes through the use of smart (and remote) service concepts. The firm is also providing financing, educational, and uptime guaranty services (see *Figure 13* for an overview of the services provided by Siemens Healthcare Systems).

### 3.3.3 *Viessmann – World leader in climate control systems*

For over 80 years Viessmann has been a highly respected player in the heating industry. From the beginning Viessmann has been one of the primary drivers of innovation in the industry and even today some of the earliest innovations of the firm are industry standards. The firm has gradually expanded its product portfolio and today has one of the most comprehensive ranges of climate control products. From small single-room apartments, large housing blocks, commercial, and industrial buildings to local heating networks the firm has the right system solution.

The firm offers individual heating systems for every type of fuel and every application involving heating and/or air-conditioning technology, as well as an extensive range of services. These include traditional floor-standing and wall-hung boilers, hot water, and electric heating appliances as well as state-of-the-art (environmentally friendly) solar thermal collectors, heat pumps, micro combined heat and power plants, and condensing and biomass boilers.

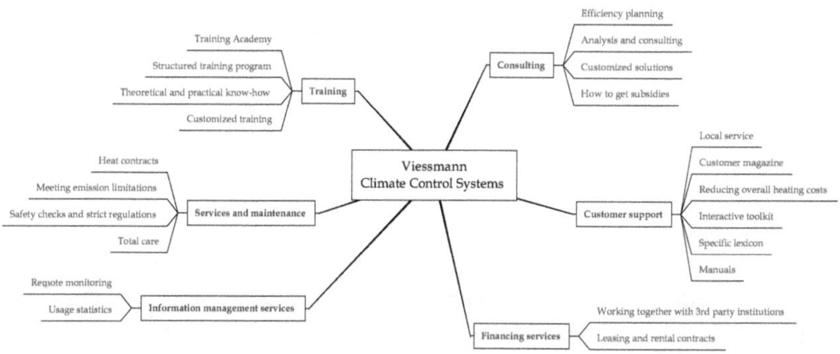


*Figure 14: Mind map: Viessmann climate control systems*

The firm - headquartered in Europe, with over 15 production sites worldwide and a presence in over 100 countries - is a leading world player in the industry. The firm has built a leading reputation for quality, design, and innovation in the industry. In the past 10 to 15 years the firm has focused on developing its service offerings. The firm has developed different service offerings for different geographical markets. Typically, services for end customers (homeowners) focus on reducing their heating bills. On the other hand, services for installers (the typical client in many markets) focus on expanding the business of an installer (i.e. helping acquire more end-customers). The firm also provides a range of remote monitoring services using information and communication technologies (see *Figure 14* for an overview of the services provided by Viessmann Climate Control Systems).

### 3.3.4 Wetrok – European leader in cleaning systems

Wetrok, founded over 50 years ago, is a pioneer in cleaning technology. Since its inception the firm has continued to collaborate with the cleaning industry and has developed a comprehensive range of technologically advanced professional cleaning machines. These include scrubber driers, road sweepers, wet and dry vacuums, single brush machines, and litter vacuums to transport trolleys, consumables, cleaning chemicals, and accessories.

*Figure 15: Mind map: Wetrok cleaning systems*

The firm, a leader in the European market, has employees in over 30 countries and supplies over 85,000 customers worldwide. Wetrok, well known for the exceptional quality of its products, competes in the premium product segment. The firm claims that it manufactures things to have a long lifespan and promises to outlast and outperform the competition. Changing and challenging client demands are seen as an opportunity by Wetrok. These have resulted in innovative solutions, product innovations, and new service processes. In the process the firm has set new industry standards. The core clients of Wetrok are professional cleaning firms and large central enterprises such as airports, hospitals, and hotels. In the last decade, the firm introduced monthly fee-based service plans through which customers have access to a 24/7 repair service network. These round the clock technicians are equipped with spare parts so that asset availability is not adversely affected. In addition the firm has actively moved into preventive maintenance, shop floor advice, and consumable checks (see *Figure 15* for an overview of the services provided by Wetrok Cleaning Systems).

# 4 Findings

The in-depth cross case analysis of the case studies throws light on two main goals of this study. First, it recognizes how firms endeavor to improve the value proposition they offer to their customer. Here five distinct services are identified that support extant solution-based business model literature. Second, it demonstrates that firms through solution-based business models aim at strategic innovation. For this the innovation framework of Kim and Mauborgne (2005) has been used. These two aspects are discussed below.

## 4.1 Towards a New Value Proposition: Five Distinct Services

Five distinct services provided by firms in the capital goods industry in their quest to improve the value proposition they offer to their customers are identified. The five services form the basis of improving the buyer value. By providing these services, these firms are slowly but steadily moving from being traditional product sellers to being services providers.

### *4.1.1 Business consulting*

All four firms had extensively developed their business consulting capabilities and viewed business consulting as a crucial and core service component of their offering. It should be noted that business consulting had expanded from being specific to the product portfolio to being industry specific. Viessmann provided consulting to end clients (home owners) to define requirements and advise them on ways to increase heating efficiency. Wetrok consulted its clients not only on the extent of resources required to clean and maintain large facilities, but also provided a plan on how to efficiently execute the cleaning process. Similarly, Electrolux and Siemens provided a broad range of consulting services. They helped their customers understand their needs better and designed customized solutions to meet customer needs on a pin point basis. They examined the entire process, determined the requirements, and the layout of equipment required. Siemens also provided business consulting to optimize internal customer response processes to identify and eliminate resource wastefulness. It also came to light that the firms had begun to charge for the business consulting service in the past few years. As one manager stated:[13]

> *"If a service can only thrive by itself when it is provided free, then probably the service has no value."*

Another manager had similar views and stated:

> *"If the customer is willing to pay for it, only then you know that the particular service makes sense and should be persisted with."*

Even though some were still giving parts of the business consulting services for free, the managers said that the not-for-free rationale was still followed in principle. Their decision not to charge was clearly conveyed to the customer on the invoice as a discount provided. For instance, one of the managers stated:

> *"… now then if you decide to give it for free anyway, that's another issue, that's ok. But the customer needs to appreciate the benevolence shown."*

### 4.1.2 *Comprehensive services*

The analysis reveals that all the four firms were looking to develop their standard repair and maintenance offerings to comprehensive services. In some cases they had gone a step further and were guaranteeing uptime of their assets. Wetrok has two models of comprehensive contracts based on ownership. In the first, the customer buys the asset and pays a monthly service (for the minimum duration of a year) on top of the purchase for guaranteed maximum lead time (guaranteed SLA) in case of asset failure. In the second model the customer does not buy the machine but pays a monthly fee to have the asset available for use. The second model was not successful as the assets were misused by the customer. In brief, the lack of asset ownership led to dysfunctional customer behavior. Viessmann, with the help of 3rd party firms, was also providing heat-contracts. In such heat-contracts the supplier promises to keep a facility warm for a fixed monthly charge, i.e. sells heat to the customer. The complete responsibility from financing the assets to operating them was taken over by the supplier. Siemens was actively marketing its uptime services (guaranteed asset availability) to the end customers. As one manager stated:

> *"Uptime services are in many cases too futuristic for our customers. Hence we let them (customers) decide to what extent they sign up for such service contracts. In many cases customers decide to be more adventurous as time passes and opt for guaranteed outcomes in a long run."*

[13] A full list of interview citations is provided in Annex B.

Another manager responsible for pioneering of a state-of-the-art technology said,

> *"The main service is uptime service. We provide the customer about 90% of availability. We say within a maximum of ten hours' knock down the machine runs again. We guarantee a sort of patient throughput. We guarantee that you can treat at least for example twenty patients a day. That is what we guarantee. Failure is expensive for us as we have to then pay financial penalties."*

Electrolux has also developed its uptime service guarantee program. As one manger stated,

> *"... most do not understand the numbers behind the success of a service organization. Ten preventive maintenance visits cost less than one machine failure."*

Today, for a fixed charge the firm takes over complete responsibility for the proper functioning of machines.

### 4.1.3 *Educational services*

Educational services have become an important service offering in all four firms. Barely existent a decade ago, except in the case of Viessmann, it is an important revenue generator in all the four firms. According to a manager working at Wetrok:

> *"Cleaning is an art and a science. It is a profession. It is not something everyone can do, but it can be taught systematically in classroom. And once we realized the potential we started a cleaning academy."*

The firm has taken educational services very seriously and trains close to 4,000 people every year. The firm provides training from the person that does the actual cleaning at the bottom end, all the way up to the business leader/manager of the whole setup. Viessmann has taken education services seriously for the past 40+ years and set up an academy as long ago as the 1960s. According to the firm, the academy has been a pillar of the firm's philosophy since then. Today over 70,000 people take part in training each year. The training courses are based on hands-on experience backed up through expert tuition courses. The training is developed to improve the skills of installers and keep them abreast with the latest technologies and practices in the heating industry. The firm today is the industry's leading training provider in Europe. Siemens has a long tradition of providing training to its customers. As and when Siemens introduced state-of-the-art products in the healthcare industry it had to simultaneously provide training to the people who operated the machines on a pro bono basis for the first time. However, when an operator was replaced the new operator also had to be trained to use the machine. Seeing an opportunity here, Siemens in the recent past has systematically monetized its training offerings. The firm was also training the operators to be first level technicians so that they can solve the most common problems themselves. Electrolux believes that laundry is a science and professional washers need to be taught the tricks of the trade to clean better and efficiently. The firm has developed an extensive range of training programs as it believes that the best solution can be worthless, unless the people involved know how to use the equipment optimally. These training programs include, for example, information on taking proper care of different textiles, different laundry methods and techniques, and knowledge about the quality of water and detergents.

#### *4.1.4 Financing services*

Our research showed that all four firms are providing financial services to their customers. Wetrok cooperated with local third-party financial institutions to provide finance to its clients. Loans arranged from such institutions generally ranged between 5,000 to 50,000 Euros. The manager stated that:

> *"We do some leasing, but to be honest, we don't do a lot because it's not attractive for us. This is really not our competency. Saying this, we rather work with third parties who provide the required financial solution. Be it loans or leasing contracts. Something we ourselves do, if we are required to providing a leasing contract."*

Viessmann also worked with third-party financial institutions to provide both loans and leasing contracts. Siemens has taken a complete plunge into providing financing solutions for its clients. They have a dedicated financial department which effectively is a financial institution and provides a comprehensive range of financial services. One interviewee said:

> *"... the company philosophy is that all should benefit from breakthroughs in medical technology. We finance well, it is our competitive advantage."*

For each customer - be it a small privately run clinic with 10 beds or a mega hospital with over 2,000 beds - the firm provides the most appropriate financial solution to make technology affordable. Financial solutions include paying on a "per scan" basis, hire purchase, structured term loans, structured finance lease, leasing, and rental arrangements. The firm also provides insurance against technology obsoleteness through its equipment and technology upgrade packages. Electrolux has also recognized the virtues of providing vendors with finance. Customers can choose from a variety of leasing, rental, and loan contracts. In some markets (countries) the firm has partnered with financial institutions to provide financing solutions.

### *4.1.5 Information management services*

With the advances in ICT technologies in the past decade, all four firms have seriously looked at realizing the benefits of information management. Electrolux, for example, developed software that helps customers collect operating statistics such as the running hours, idle time, temperatures, residual moisture, and consumption of water, detergent, and energy for their machines. With such statistics you can customize programs for specific wash needs for different garments. One manager stated:

> *"… for example, with the help of usage statistics and experience you can optimize the temperature at which you want to wash or compress the length of wash programs, while still maintaining or improving quality standards."*

Another manager stated:

> *"Considerable cost saving can be realized by optimizing washing programs."*

With a mouse click one can program the machine to run at a customized specification. The program can also be used to efficiently schedule batches to improve running time. Siemens also offers an advanced information management packages that is similar to an enterprise resource planning (ERP) package. The powerful software package helps plan, control, and execute the whole workflow involved in providing healthcare. From organizing patient schedules, monitoring waiting lists, maintaining patient records, consulting the doctor in his diagnosis to billing, the software based on best case practices eliminates wastages and diminishes human error. Viessmann offers a premium after-sales package which allows one to remotely control (via the internet) home heating systems. The statistics collected by the system can also help maximize energy savings. In some markets, using similar technologies, the firm is also taking over running of heating systems. Wetrok is currently experimenting with such services. One interviewee stated:

> *"There is a lot of potential as technology moves forward. The machines can communicate back to you and tell you things, tell you how many chemicals they used, how much they worked and where the problems are. You can identify faults before they cause any work disruption."*

The manager also discussed the advantages of integrating a global positioning system for tracking the movement of the cleaning machines. He further stated:

> *"... another option is of course to use indoor GPS, you could track the machines and you could provide a history of what they have done. This information could be very valuable. Especially as customers outsource cleaning to a contractor they want to monitor the contractor. The contractors find it attractive as they can not only monitor their employees but also provide proof to their clients of their work."*

## 4.2 Solution-based Business Model as Strategic Innovation

In the previous section five distinct services are identified. These complementary services help firms provide marketing-integration to their customers. As discussed previously in part III, marketing-integration is the main value creating attribute for the cluster of solutions. Even though marketing-integration may create value for the customer; it may not translate into profit for the supplying firm. For escaping, this hybrid value creation paradox of an increase in total revenues, but a decrease in profitability as a percentage of total sales (Neely 2008), there has to be sound reasoning behind the services offered by firms.

This study helps identify that firms, by adding these services, should aim at strategic innovation of their business models. The analysis shows that the underlying principle for a successful solution-based business model is similar to that of value innovation (Kim and Mauborgne 2005). In both cases, a firm's innovations aim at achieving two things simultaneously:

1. increasing the buyer value;
2. reducing the cost structure of their offerings.

These two seemingly contradictory goals are discussed in the following two sections and graphically represented in *Figure 16*.

### *4.2.1 Increasing buyer value*

Increasing buyer value, the first goal, is achieved by innovatively combining services to their products. In all four cases, business consulting services were further developed and branded (sold with an emphasis) as a value creating service. Firms claimed that they could bring in their knowledge of the industry to improve the internal processes of their customers. All four firms were willing to provide comprehensive service contracts where they took over risk from their customers. For example, Viessmann with its heat-contracts is now responsible to keep their customers warm. Siemens, Electrolux, and Wetrok with their uptime service contracts, with inbuilt penalties if the agreed SLAs were not met, have taken over the risk from their customers.

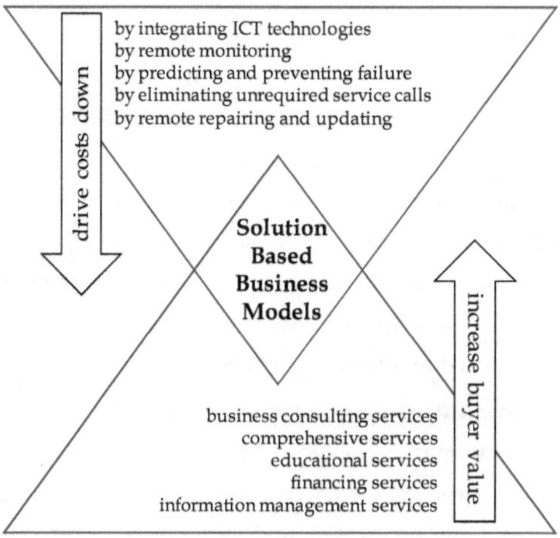


*Figure 16: Solution-based business model and the value innovation framework (based on Kim and Mauborgne 2005)*

Educational and financial services are identified as service innovations. Educational services have become an important source of revenue in all four firms. Not surprisingly the firms have come up with structured learning programs for all levels of management. Financial services also create buyer value. For example, in the case of Siemens, the ingenious "pay per scan" revenue model, provided by an independent finance department, helps small hospitals expand their business. Finally, information management services based on embedded ICT technologies are leading to a media-rich channel between the machines, the suppliers, and the customers. This in turn facilitates better monitoring of assets, customer behavior, and supplier commitment leading to innovative customer-service processes. In the process of providing new services, firms were repositioning themselves as solution providers or as customer partners. Such a shift from the old to the new value proposition also demanded a paradigm shift in how firms frame *what they do*. Firms have not only developed strong service organizations to successfully migrate to providing solutions, but have also redefined the business they are in. This has led to them moving from a seller *"we-sell-products"* mindset to a partner *"we-help-you-do-better"* mindset. There is a change not only in the context in which offers are introduced, but also in the underlying mental models which frame what a firm does.

### *4.2.2 Reducing cost structures*

Reducing the cost structure, the second goal, is simultaneously pursued by all four firms. Costs associated with providing the added services were kept in check. Firstly, firms focused on services that were based on their existing knowledge and competencies. For example, business consulting services, comprehensive services, educational services, and information management services were directly based on exploiting the intensive tacit knowledge firms have of their products and industry. This is also supported in the cross case analysis, where it is noticed that financing services are always[14] provided in association with third-party financial institutions because firms lacked knowhow to provide them.

At the same time, firms also focus on leveraging new technologies to drive down costs. For example, by integrating ICT technologies into machines, firms are coming up with novel service processes such as remote monitoring. Such services are helping firms cut costs by predicting and preventing asset failure, eliminating unrequired service, repairing, and updating products remotely. In other words, firms are using the latest technologies to reduce wastages and improve service processes. In some cases, products with large software components - for example a CT scan machine - are not only monitored, but also repaired and updated remotely. In addition, it is noticed that all four firms are considering repair convenience when designing products. The logic is clear, as firms promise uptime guarantee services; it is in their interest that the machines are easy (and quick) to repair.

[14] In the case of Siemens, the financing services are provided by an independent Siemens organization. It is considered as a third-party financial institution as its core competency is to provide financial services to the clients of Siemens.

# 5 Reflection

In general, this empirical study explores solutions, a cluster of hybrid value creation business models, in the context of the capital goods industry. Specifically, it focuses on understanding how firms can achieve profitability through a solution-based business model. It identifies that manufacturing firms, which are successful in providing solutions, engage in strategic innovation by providing a host of services that are built around their traditional products. In the process, manufacturing firms are not only providing an increased level of marketing-integration to their customers, but also repositioning themselves from sellers of products to solvers of customer problems. The findings of this study have both theoretical and practical implications.

On a theoretical level, the findings support the existing research on solution-based business models. First, as suggested by Allmendinger and Lombreglia (2005), solution-based business models do revolve around the life cycle of a product. Even in cases where a firm becomes a service provider, all the high-value services it provides are built around its traditional product. On a related note the findings support, as suggested by Sharma and Molloy (1999), that solution-based business models should help customers achieve better outcomes. As shown in the four case studies, these firms are helping their customers: (1) improve their operating performance through information management and business consulting services, (2) increase their asset effectiveness by providing educational services, (3) expand their market by providing financial services, and (4) mitigate risks by providing comprehensive services. In the process, as suggested by Harrison (2003), the firms are becoming an educational, diagnostic, and discovery providers for their customers.

On a practical level, this study shows that firms that want to succeed in a solution-based business model need to follow a hybrid strategy. Firms need to not only focus on increasing buyer value by meeting their needs better, but also on reducing costs by eliminating resource wastefulness. As shown in the case studies, firms make use of state-of-art technologies to exploit their tacit knowledge (of both their products and the industry) to meet these goals that seem to be, but are not contradictory. In situations where they lack certain competencies (e.g. in financing) firms should be open to working with third parties to augment their offer.

The strengths of this study must be tempered with recognition of its limitations. The sample consisting of four case studies is relatively small and does not offer an exhaustive assortment of organizations. On a similar note, the interviewee sample was limited in size, which is a common trade-off in qualitative research. The method used was fitting, since the goal of this study was to capture depth of understanding rather than breadth at this explorative phase. Also, in case study research generalization is gained in terms of generalizing findings to theory rather than to a large population (Eisenhardt 1989; Yin 2003).

In conclusion, this empirical study contributes to a better understanding of solution-based business model innovation in the context of firms that produce standardized capital goods in large volumes. In sum, the findings propose that these firms need to exploit the tacit knowledge they have with regard to their products and the industry to provide services better and cheaper. They do not have to choose between one of the two generic strategies proposed by Porter (1998), but can differentiate, and at the same time can continue to compete on the basis of costs.

# VI

# Discussion and Conclusion

# 1 Summary and Contribution

This dissertation deals with hybrid value creation, i.e., the process of generating additional value by innovatively combining products (tangible components) and services (intangible components). It is identified, as seen from the different examples such as the *PoshBags4rent, MyMuesli, Flexpetz, Hilti, Kindle, miCoach,* and *Rolls-Royce,* that there are many unique ways of combining products and services to create new offerings. All the above-mentioned examples fall into one of the four clusters of hybrid value creation - *embedded products, leasing & co., mass customization* and *solutions* - developed in this dissertation. Overall, this dissertation focuses on understanding the dynamics of value creation in the diverse business models of hybrid value creation. This chapter provides a summary along with the contributions of parts I to VI. Chapter 2 provides a holistic view of the managerial implications based on the results of the encompassing research studies. Finally, directions for future research, intended to inspire future research, are presented in chapter 3.

**Summary and contributions of parts I to VI**

In part I, first the definition of *hybrid value creation* as the process of generating additional value by innovatively combining products (tangible components) and services (intangible components) was systematically derived. In addition, the relevance of hybrid value creation in practice was elucidated. Here it was recognized that more and more firms are shifting their focus from offering standalone products or services towards offering integrated combinations of products and services to better meet the specific demands of customers. It was also identified that the phenomenon of combining products and services covers a wide range of industries and is relevant in both the business-to-business and business-to-customer contexts.

In part II, a state-of-the-art report on hybrid value creation was provided. This was required because extant research in the field is fragmented, due to researchers from different disciplines and countries using different terms to describe the same phenomenon. To bring together findings from different strands of research conducted into one document, this literature review systematically identified and then analyzed 169 publications in the field. These publications were classified into eight categories: (1) the *strategic view;* (2) the *organization view;* (3) the *marketing view;*

(4) the *design view*; (5) the *innovation view*; (6) the *business level view*; (7) *sustainability aspects*; and (8) the *macroeconomic perspective*. Research in each of these categories was summarized. Based on their links and interactions, a first categorization of the field is developed and presented. It also provided a discussion and reflected on the findings with respect to the pervasiveness of literature and the research methods used. It concluded with the identification of some dominant strategic gaps in the overall research landscape and provided directions for future research. One dominant strategic gap identified was to understand how and where value in different business models of hybrid value creation was created. This question was looked into detail in the following part.

Part III focused on answering the research question: how and where is value created in different business models of hybrid value creation? *Table 29* provides a summary of part III. To achieve this, first, four value creating attributes from theory - *individualization, marketing-integration, operational-integration,* and *firm-customer interaction* - were identified. Second, using a deductive case analysis four distinct clusters of hybrid value creation business models - *embedded products, leasing & co., mass customization,* and *solutions* - were developed. This was done (required) because it did not make sense to compare a simple car rental service with a complex turnkey project, both examples of hybrid value creation. A cross cluster analysis was conducted on the four clusters to identify the role and impact of the identified value creating attributes. By doing this, the key value creating attribute for each cluster was identified. As a result, this study suggested a two-step strategy to increase the success of hybrid offerings. When implementing hybrid value creation: (1) the type of hybrid value creation has to be determined, and firms can do this by identifying to which one of the four clusters their offering belongs; (2) depending on the cluster, the corresponding key value creating attribute needs to be carefully designed. Finally, two clusters - *embedded products* and *solutions* - are identified to entail further research. The other two clusters - *leasing & co.* and *mass customization* - are identified to have grown into independent research subjects and hence are no more a focus of this dissertation.

*Table 29: Summary of part III*

| ***Part III - Empirical Study 1: The Four Clusters of Hybrid Value Creation*** | | | | |
|---|---|---|---|---|
| ***Challenge*** | Even though firms have identified the potential of hybrid value creation, they are still not sure what factors really create value in different hybrid value creation business models | | | |
| ***Research question*** | How and where is value created in different business models of hybrid value creation? | | | |
| ***From theory*** | Four value creating attributes - individualization, marketing-integration, operational-integration, and firm–customer interaction - identified | | | |
| ***Four clusters formed using deductive case analysis*** | **Embedded products** | **Leasing & co.** | **Mass customization** | **Solutions** |
| ***Method used*** | **Cross cluster analysis** | | | |
| ***Results*** *(Main value creating attribute for each cluster identified)* | **Operational-integration** | **Individualization** | **Operational-integration** | **Marketing-integration** |
| ***Implications*** | **Suggested a two-step strategy to increase the success of hybrid offerings** | | | |
| ***Further outlook*** | Led to research question that is addressed in part IV | Directs readers to other existing research | Directs readers to other existing research | Led to research question that is addressed in part V |

Parts IV and V followed up on the findings of part III. *Table 30* provides a summary of both the parts.

*Table 290: Summaries of parts IV and V*

| | ***Part IV – Empirical Study 2***<br>***The Cluster of Embedded Products*** | ***Part V – Empirical Study 3***<br>***The Cluster of Solutions*** |
|---|---|---|
| ***Builds on*** | Part III, where operational-integration is identified as the key value creating attribute for this cluster | Part III, where marketing-integration is identified as the key value creating attribute for this cluster |
| ***Challenge*** | Embedded products need to be immaculately designed | Solution-based business models need to improve the value proposition they offer to their customer |
| ***Research question*** | What are the critical aspects that need to be taken into consideration when designing an embedded product? | What should be the logic behind a firm's strategy to implement a solution-based business model? |
| ***Method used*** | Explorative qualitative case study method | Explorative qualitative case study method |
| ***Sample*** | Six firms that offered distinct embedded products: an e-book reader, fitness machines, a gaming console, a music player, a programmable toy, and a web-based personal trainer | Four international firms operating in different industries: laundry systems *(Electrolux)*, healthcare systems *(Siemens)*, climate control systems *(Viessmann)*, and cleaning systems *(Wetrok)* |
| ***Results*** | Six critical aspects that influence the design of embedded products are identified | The identification of five distinct services and the underlying principle for a solution-based business model is similar to that of value innovation |
| ***Implications*** | For the successful design of embedded products, firms need to look at embedded product not just as a bundling strategy, but as an innovation strategy | To be successful with a solution-based business model, firms need to follow a hybrid strategy. To achieve this, firms need to exploit their tacit knowledge to provide services better and cheaper |

Part IV focused on answering the research question: what are the critical aspects that need to be taken into consideration when designing an embedded product? This question builds on the research undertaken in part III, where operational-integration was identified as the key value creating attribute and success factor for the cluster of embedded products. Hence, it is imperative that offerings from this cluster are immaculately designed. To identify the critical aspects an explorative qualitative case study approach was used. Unstructured interviews were conducted with 12 product developers and/or marketing managers from six firms that offered distinct embedded products: an *e-book reader, fitness machines*, a *gaming console*, a *music player*, a *programmable toy*, and a *web-based personal trainer*. Analysis and iterative comparison of the data identified six critical aspects that should be taken into consideration. Three critical aspects - *hybrid arrangement, dimension of hybridity,* and *revenue model used* - were strategically-oriented. Three other critical aspects - *the web as a service platform, engagement in community building,* and *integration of customer feedback* - were service-oriented. The findings advise firms that for the successful design of embedded products, they need to think about the embedded product not just as a bundling strategy, but as an innovation strategy. Overall, the findings show that firms did not really know how to integrate the service dimension to use it as a driver for value creation.

Part V focused on answering the research question: what should be the logic behind a firm's strategy to implement a solution-based business model? This question builds on the research undertaken in part III, where marketing-integration was identified as the key value creating attribute for offerings from this cluster. This study builds on existing theoretical contributions by drawing from exploratory case study research undertaken with four international firms operating in different industries: laundry systems *(Electrolux)*, healthcare systems *(Siemens)*, climate control systems *(Viessmann)*, and cleaning systems *(Wetrok)*. Primary data was collected through multiple interviews conducted with at least two managers working in sales and/ or service and/ or commercial departments of the selected firms. A cross case analysis identified five distinct service offerings: *business consulting services, comprehensive services, educational services, financial services,* and *information management services.* In sum, the analysis reveals that to be successful in a solution-based business model, firms need to aim for strategic innovation, i.e., firms need to follow a hybrid strategy. They need to focus not only on increasing buyer value by meeting customer needs better, but also on reducing cost structures by eliminating resource wastefulness. To achieve these contradictory goals, firms need to exploit their tacit knowledge of their products and industry.

Part VI concludes this dissertation by providing a summary of contributions. In addition it provides a holistic view of the implications for practice and directions for future research based on the results of the four encompassing research studies. These are presented in the following two chapters.

# 2 Managerial Implications

This dissertation has focused on deciphering the value creation dynamics in the context of hybrid value creation. Based on the results of the three empirical studies, this chapter helps managers gain a better understanding of how they can be successful in creating value through product–service combinations. To achieve this, in the first step, managerial implications are developed around the following two questions:

1. What is my product–service offering all about?
2. How and where is value created in my product-service offerings?

*What is my product–service offering all about?*

It is important that managers understand what their product–service offering is all about. In other words, it is crucial that managers are conscious of what they want to achieve through their hybrid offerings. To accomplish this, managers need to relate their offering to one of the four clusters of hybrid value creation. These are:

1. *Embedded products*: where the primary goal of a combined offering is to create a new offering or protect an existing product from competition by enhancing it with embedded services using digital technologies;
2. *Leasing & co.:* where the primary goal is to expand the market for capital intensive (sometimes relative) products by providing them to customers on rental- or use-basis;
3. *Mass customization:* where the primary goal is to provide an individualized product to end customers at a reasonable premium;
4. *Solutions:* where the primary goal is to help customers focus on their core competencies and not on non-core activities.

Once this is achieved, managers should then focus on the next question, dealing with how and where value is created in their offering.

*How and where is value created in my product–service offerings?*

To help mangers get a grasp of how and where value is created in different clusters of product–service offerings, four diverse value creating attributes are identified from literature and their contribution for the different clusters of hybrid value creation is empirically derived. *Table 31* presents the most crucial value creating attribute for each cluster. In addition, it explains how value is created through the most crucial value creating attribute for each cluster.

*Table 31: Overview of crucial value creating attributes for each cluster*

| Cluster | Crucial value creating attribute | Value is created through: |
|---|---|---|
| Embedded products | Operational-integration | The seamless technical-integration of hardware and software aspects. |
| Leasing & co. | Individualization | The individualization of contract volume, i.e., customers can choose how long they use a product and how many products they can use at a time. |
| Mass customization | Operational-integration | The online configurator that helps customers define and convey their needs to the supplier. |
| Solutions | Marketing-integration | Consolidated vendor accountability that is provided through a range of complementary services that are offered by suppliers. |

This helps managers identify the crucial value creating attribute they need to focus on depending on the cluster their offerings belongs to. For example, if a firm is active in the cluster of embedded products, it is imperative that it first focuses on the value creating attribute 'operational-integration'. Once this attribute is appropriately addressed, then the firm should also look at the remaining value attributes. As a result, a two-step strategy to increase the success of hybrid offerings is suggested. When implementing hybrid value creation:

1. The type of hybrid value creation has to be determined. Firms can do this by identifying to which one of the four clusters their offering belongs to.
2. Depending on the cluster, the corresponding key value creating attribute needs to be carefully designed.

In the second step, the managerial implications focusing on two clusters - *embedded products* and *solutions* - that were further studied are provided. These are developed around the following two questions:

1. What should be kept in mind when designing an embedded product?
2. What should be the logic behind a firm's strategy to implement a solution-based business model?

*What should one keep in mind when designing an embedded product?*

Managers need to recognize the importance of aligning the strategic and the service components of their embedded products. For example, the revenue model needs to be designed in such a way that it supports customer acceptance of the service component in the context of the whole offer. By not taking such an approach, while designing an embedded product, firms are primed to fail with their offerings in the market. In total, four important managerial implications are provided, which are:

1. Managers need to go beyond their applied 'trial-and-error strategy' when designing embedded products.
2. Managers need to think about the embedded product not as a bundling strategy, but as an innovation strategy.
3. Managers need to think outside the box to come up with novel embedded products. This means that managers need to look outside the traditional value chain to identify products and services to combine. This way firms can design radically new embedded products and thus create new markets.
4. Managers need to integrate customers in the design process. This is also identified as a direction for future research and discussed in the next chapter.

*What should be the logic behind a firm's strategy to implement a solution-based business model?*

Managers are advised that a move into a solution-based business model will only be successful if they can achieve strategic innovation when combining products and services into a solution. Using the value innovation framework, this study shows that firms that want to succeed in a solution-based business model need to follow a hybrid strategy, i.e., firms need to focus not only on increasing buyer value by meeting their needs better, but also reduce costs by eliminating resource wastefulness. To achieve this, the following managerial suggestions are made:

1. Managers should focus on providing services that are based on their existing knowledge and competencies. For example, business consulting services, comprehensive services, educational services, and information management services are directly based on exploiting the intensive tacit knowledge firms have of their products and industry.
2. Managers should be open to work with external organizations if they lack certain competencies. For example, all four firms in the sample collaborated with a third-party financial institution to provide financial services because they lacked the competencies to provide such services themselves.
3. Managers, wherever possible, should make use of state-of-art technologies to exploit their tacit knowledge (of both their products and the industry). For example, remote monitoring (using ICT) can not only help firms to improve the value proposition by predicting and preventing failure, but also reduce cost structures by eliminating unrequired service calls.

In sum, these managerial suggestions are designed to guide managers to succeed in their endeavor to create value by combining products and services.

# 3 Directions for Future Research

Any research journey would be incomplete without providing *'directions for future research'*, which help in identifying and building research on a particular subject or phenomenon. Management research is a conversation between scholars to further knowledge and understanding of any given phenomenon (Huff 2009). In line with this, on one hand this dissertation has built on research gaps identified by other scholars; on the other hand, it concludes by identifying research gaps that are deemed important to further the knowledge on phenomenon of hybrid value creation. This chapter brings together future research directions identified in this dissertation. They are presented below.

Analysis conducted on 169 publications identified in the systematic literature review revealed that there has been a limited use of theory. This lack of extensive theoretical underpinning can largely be attributed to the fact that a considerable part of research has been conducted by researchers from the disciplines of engineering and operations. These are disciplines where the use of theory and theory-building is not the primary focus of research. One must also add that even studies from the management side have made limited use of theory. There is, however, a clear preference to using the service-dominant logic. This can be seen as authors often focus on meeting customer problems or solving specific customer needs. This is also supported by the fact that the definitions of many terms identifying with hybrid value creation make explicit reference to meeting customer needs (see *Table 2* – presented previously in part II). In addition to the service-dominant logic, researchers in the area of hybrid value creation seem to rather build on a resource-based than on a market-based view. There is clear inclination to use the resource-based view to identify firm readiness for hybrid value creation. Extant research argues that firms need specific capabilities and resources to be successful with hybrid value creation. Even though the resource-based view is an important lens to look at firm readiness for hybrid value creation, a dynamic capabilities view would be more appropriate. This is because an evolutionary view of firm resources and capabilities complementing the static perspective provided by the resource-based view is argued to be more suitable to understand the struggles faced by firms moving into hybrid value creation. The firm which can build, integrate, and reconfigure both internal and external competencies to address the needs of their customers the fastest (and of course adequately) will be most successful with hybrid value creation. Therefore it is proposed that future research should focus on understanding how firms can go about achieving success with hybrid value creation. In addition, the systematic literature review identified gaps in each of the eight categories that are listed in the *Table 32* below. For more information the reader should refer to part II.

*Table 302: Research gaps identified in the systematic literature review*

| Category of research | Some important gaps identified for future research |
|---|---|
| *Strategic view* | ▪ How and to what extent does hybrid value creation change the competitive dynamics of a firm?<br>▪ How does competition react when a firm makes a foray into hybrid value creation? |
| *Organization view* | ▪ How do internal processes, people, structures, and rewards interact with each other in the context of hybrid value creation?<br>▪ To what extent does an organization need to change to be successful in hybrid value creation? |
| *Marketing view* | ▪ How should the value of hybrid offerings be quantified?<br>▪ How should the value of hybrid offerings be communicated to the customer? |
| *Design view* | ▪ To what extent does design for product-service offerings differ from that for traditional standalone offerings?<br>▪ How to integrate and moderate stakeholder interaction in the context of designing hybrid offerings? |
| *Innovation view* | ▪ How should firms search for and select from ideas to engage in hybrid value creation?<br>▪ Research should also look at hybrid value creation as a whole phenomenon. As currently research is split into two independent streams: product innovation and service innovation. |
| *Business level view* | ▪ Research should be conducted to understand the dynamics of hybrid value creation in different industries. |
| *Sustainability aspects* | ▪ How to overcome "human craving for ownership" for the acceptance of product-service offerings in the business-to-customer sector? |
| *Macroeconomic perspective* | ▪ What role should the state play in fostering the acceptance of hybrid value creation?<br>▪ What existing policies and procedures discourage the acceptance of hybrid value creation? |

Research conducted in *empirical study 1* provided an organizational perspective to the question how and where value is created in different business models of hybrid value creation. Hence, follow-up research is required that provides a customer perspective on hybrid value creation. Some of the most important questions that need to be answered are:

1. In the context of hybrid value creation, what creates value in the eyes of the customer?
2. How can this value be measured?

It is obvious that for competitive advantage, high value needs to be delivered to customers. To understand this from a customer perspective, further research should build on literature on perceived value, as it is significantly related to customer behavior and willingness to pay (e.g. Anderson and Narus 1998; Eggert and Ulaga 2002).

Findings from *empirical study 2* emphasized the need to look at embedded products as an innovation strategy to create new markets and new lines of products; thereby supporting previous research conducted by Möslein and Kölling (2007). Also, the findings acknowledged the advantages of integrating customers in the design process of embedded products. Even though a lot of research has been conducted to understand the role of the customer in the innovation process (e.g. von Hippel 1986; Chesbrough 2003; Baldwin, Hienerth, and von Hippel 2006; Füller et al. 2006; Hienerth 2006; Lettl, Herstatt, and Gemuenden 2006; Prügl and Schreier 2006; Reichwald and Piller 2009), it has received limited attention in the context of embedded products. Hence, future research should aim to study how different tools and strategies known from the open innovation literature, such as lead user method (von Hippel 1986; Lüthje and Herstatt 2004) or idea contests (Piller and Walcher 2006), can be applied in the context of embedded products.

Finally, findings from *empirical study 3* support the existing research that solution-based business models do revolve around the life cycle of a product (Allmendinger and Lombreglia 2005). Even in case a firm becomes a service provider, all the high-value services it provides are built around its traditional product. In addition, results showed that firms that want to succeed in a solution-based business model need to follow a hybrid strategy. Firms need to focus not only on increasing buyer value by meeting their needs better, but also reduce costs by eliminating resource wastefulness. This is explained using the value innovation framework of Kim and Mauborgne (2005). This study, however, does not identify obstacles that inhibit firms in making a successful transition to a solution-based business model. This along with paths to mitigate these obstacles is identified as a relevant direction for future research. It will further help firms escape the hybrid value creation paradox – an increase in total revenues with a decrease in profitability as a percentage of total sales – as identified by Neely (2008).

**Parting comment**

It is evident that hybrid value creation is a growing phenomenon both in research and in practice. The findings of this dissertation add only one – albeit important – piece of the jigsaw puzzle that is 'hybrid value creation'. The research conducted encourages further investigation in this field of research by exploring and explaining the value creation dynamics of hybrid value creation.

# References

Acha, V.L., Brusoni, S., and Prencipe, A., 2007. Exploring the miracle: strategy and management of the knowledge base in the aeronautics industry. International Journal of Innovation and Technology Management, 4(1), 15-39.

Acha, V.L., Davies, A., Hobday, M., and Salter, A., 2004. Exploring the capital goods economy: complex product systems in the UK. Industrial and Corporate Change, 13(3), 505-529.

Ahlert, D., Heußler, T., Michaelis, M., Möller, K., Schwab, C., and Seiter, M., 2008. Instrumente zur Quantifizierung des Kundennutzens als Basis für die Preisfindung bei hybriden Produkten. Controlling, 20(8-9), 473-479.

Ala-Risku, T., 2007. Installed base information management with industrial service operations. Paper presented at the 18th Annual Conference of Production and Operations Management Society (POMS), Dallas, USA, May 4-7, 2007.

Allmendinger, G., and Lombreglia, R., 2005. Four strategies for the age of smart services. Harvard Business Review, 83(10), 131-145.

Alonso-Rasgado, T., and Thompson, G., 2006. A rapid design process for total care product creation. Journal of Engineering Design, 17(6), 509-531.

Alonso-Rasgado, T., Thompson, G., and Elfström, B.-O., 2004. The design of functional (total care) products. Journal of Engineering Design, 15(6), 515-540.

Anderson, E.W., Fornell, C., and Rust, R., 1997. Customer satisfaction, productivity, and profitability: differences between goods and services. Marketing Science, 16(2), 129-145.

Anderson, J.C., and Narus, J.A., 1995. Capturing the value of supplementary services. Harvard Business Review, 73(1), 75-83.

Anderson, J.C., and Narus, J.A., 1998. Business marketing: understand what customers value. Harvard Business Review, 76(6), 53-65.

Ang, J., and Peterson, P.P., 1984. The leasing puzzle. The Journal of Finance, XXXIX(4), 1055-1065.

Anttonen, M., 2010. Greening from the front to the back door? A typology of chemical and resource management services. Business Strategy and the Environment, 19(3), 199-215.

Araujo, L., and Spring, M., 2006. Services, products, and the institutional structure of production. Industrial Marketing Management, 35(7), 797-805.

Auguste, B.G., Harmon, E.P., and Pandit, V., 2006. The right service strategies for product companies. The McKinsey Quarterly, (1), 41-51.

Auramo, J., and Ala-Risku, T., 2005. Challenges for going downstream. International Journal of Logistics, 8(4), 333-345.

Aurich, J.C., Fuchs, C., and Wagenknecht, C., 2006. Life cycle oriented design of technical product-service systems. Journal of Cleaner Production, 14(17), 1480-1494.

Aurich, J.C., Wolf, N., Siener, M., and Schweitzer, E., 2009. Configuration of product-service systems. Journal of Manufacturing Technology Management, 20(5), 591-605.

Azarenko, A., Roy, R., Shehab, E., and Tiwari, A., 2009. Technical product-service systems: some implications for the machine tool industry. Journal of Manufacturing Technology Management, 20(5), 700-722.

Baines, T., Lightfoot, H., Peppard, J., Johnson, M., Tiwari, A., Shehab, E., and Swink, M., 2009. Towards an operations strategy for product-centric servitization. International Journal of Operations & Production Management, 29(5), 494-519.

Baines, T.S., Lightfoot, H.W., Evans, S., Neely, A., Greenough, R., Peppard, J., Roy, R., Shehab, E., Braganza, A., Tiwari, A., Alcock, J.R., Angus, J.P., Bastl, M., Cousens, A., Irving, P., Johnson, M., Kingston, J., Lockett, H., Martinez, V., Michele, P., Tranfield, D., Walton, I.M., and Wilson, H., 2007. State-of-the-art in product-service systems. Proceedings of the Institution of Mechanical Engineers, Part B: Journal of Engineering Manufacture, 221(10), 1543-1552.

Baldwin, C., Hienerth, C., and von Hippel, E., 2006. How user innovations become commercial products: a theoretical investigation and case study. Research Policy, 35(9), 1291-1313.

Bartolomeo, M., dal Maso, D., de Jong, P., Eder, P., Groenewegen, P., Hopkinson, P., James, P., Nijhuis, L., Örninge, M., Scholl, G., Slob, A., and Zaring, O., 2003. Eco-efficient producer services-what are they, how do they benefit customers and the environment and how likely are they to develop and be extensively utilised? Journal of Cleaner Production, 11(8), 829-837.

Becker, J., Beverungen, D.F., and Knackstedt, R., 2010. The challenge of conceptual modeling for product-service systems: status-quo and perspectives for reference models and modeling languages. Information Systems and e-Business Management, 8(1), 33-66.

Becker, J., Knackstedt, R., Matzner, M., and Kröger, T., 2008. Leistungsbündel aus Produkten und Dienstleistungen - Eine Entwicklungsperspektive für ERP-System-Hersteller. Industrie Management, 24(5), 69-73.

Bennett, J., Sharma, D., and Tipping, A., 2001. Customer solutions: building a strategically aligned business model. Insights: Organization & Strategic Leadership Practice, (July), 1-6.

Berger, C., Möslein, K.M., Piller, F.T., and Reichwald, R., 2005. Co-designing modes of cooperation at the customer interface: learning from exploratory research. European Management Review, 2(1), 70-87.

Berggren, E., and Nacher, T., 2002. Introducing new products can be hazardous to your company: use the right new-solutions delivery tools. Academy of Management Executive, 30(1), 92-101.

Besch, K., 2005. Product-service systems for office furniture: barriers and opportunities on the European market. Journal of Cleaner Production, 13(10-11), 1083-1094.

Beverungen, D., Knackstedt, R., and Müller, O., 2008. Entwicklung serviceorientierter Architekturen zur Integration von Produktion und Dienstleistung - Eine Konzeptionsmethode und ihre Anwendung am Beispiel des Recyclings elektronischer Geräte. Wirtschaftsinformatik, 50(3), 220-234.

Blecker, T., and Friedrich, G., 2006. Mass customization: challenges and solutions. New York, USA: Springer.

Böhmann, T., Langer, P., and Schermann, M., 2008. Systematische Überführung von kundenspezifischen IT-Lösungen in integrierte Produkt-Dienstleistungsbausteine mit der SCORE-Methode. Wirtschaftsinformatik, 50(3), 196-207.

Bonnemeier, S., 2009. Wertschaffung und Wertaneignung als Erfolgsfaktoren von Lösungsanbietern. Wiesbaden, Germany: Gabler.

Bonnemeier, S., Buriánek, F., and Reichwald, R., 2009. Hybride Wertschöpfung - Die Fähigkeit zur Kundenintegration. Industrie Management, 25(2), 29-32.

Bonnemeier, S., Ihl, C., Buriánek, F., and Reichwald, R., 2008. Value creation and value appropriation capabilities in the context of solution selling: an exploratory study. Paper presented at the 8th European Academy of Management Conference (EURAM), Ljubljana, Slovenia, May 14-17, 2008.

Bowen, D. E., Siehl, C., and Schneider, B., 1989. A framework for analyzing customer service orientations in manufacturing. The Academy of Management Review, 14(1), 75-95.

Bower, R.S., Herringer, F.C., and Williamson, J.P., 1966. Lease evaluation. Accounting Review, 41(2), 257-265.

Bowman, C., and Ambrosini, V., 2000. Value creation versus value capture: towards a coherent definition of value in strategy. British Journal of Management, 11, 1-15.

Brady, T., and Davies, A., 2004. Building project capabilities: from exploratory to exploitative learning. Organization Studies, 25(9), 1601-1621.

Brady, T., Davies, A., and Gann, D., 2005a. Creating value by delivering integrated solutions. International Journal of Project Management, 23(5), 360-365.

Brady, T., Davies, A., and Gann, D., 2005b. Can integrated solutions business models work in construction? Building Research & Information, 33(6), 571-579.

Brax, S.A., and Jonsson, K., 2009. Developing integrated solution offerings for remote diagnostics: a comparative case study of two manufacturers. International Journal of Operations & Production Management, 29(5), 539-560.

Briceno, T., and Stagl, S., 2006. The role of social processes for sustainable consumption. Journal of Cleaner Production, 14(17), 1541-1551.

Broekhuizen, T.L.J., and Alsem, K.J., 2000. Success factors for mass customization: a conceptual model. Journal of Market-Focused Management, 5(4), 309-330.

Brown, S.W., 2000. The move to solutions providers. Marketing Management, 9(1), 10-11.

Buriánek, F., 2009. Vertragsgestaltung bei hybriden Leistungsangeboten. Wiesbaden, Germany: Gabler.

Buriánek, F., Bonnemeier, S., Ihl, C., and Reichwald, R., 2008. Erlösmodellgestaltung bei hybriden Produkten. Controlling, 20(8-9), 488-494.

Buriánek, F., Ihl, C., Bonnemeier, S., and Reichwald, R., 2007. Typologisierung hybrider Produkte. Ein Ansatz basierend auf der Komplexität der Leistungserbringung. Working paper no. 01/2007, Lehrstuhls für Betriebswirtschaftslehre - Information, Organisation und Management, TU Munich.

Ceci, F., and Prencipe, A., 2008. Configuring capabilities for integrated solutions: evidence from the IT sector. Industry & Innovation, 15(3), 277-296.

Ceschin, F., and Vezzoli, C., 2010. The role of public policy in stimulating radical environmental impact reduction in the automotive sector: the need to focus on product-service system innovation. International Journal of Automotive Technology and Management, 10(2-3), 321-341.

Chamberlain, E.H., 1962. The theory of monopolistic competition: a re-orientation of the theory of value. 8th edition, Cambridge, USA: Harvard University Press.

Chase, R.B., and Erikson, W.J., 1992. The service factory. Academy of Management, 2(3), 191-196.

Chesbrough, H., 2003. Open innovation: the new imperative for creating and profiting from technology. Boston, USA: Harvard Business School Press.

Chesbrough, H., 2007. Business model innovation: it's not just about technology anymore. Strategy & Leadership, 35(6), 12-17.

Christensen, C.M., Johnson, M.W., and Rigby, D.K., 2002. Foundations for growth: how to identify and build disruptive new businesses. MIT Sloan Management Review, 43(3), 22-31.

Cohen, M.A., Agrawal, N., and Agrawal, V., 2006. Winning in the aftermarket. Harvard Business Review, 84(5), 129-138.

Cohen, M.A., Cull, C., Lee, H.L., and Willen, D., 2000. Saturn's supply-chain innovation: high value in after-sales service. Sloan Management Review, 41(4), 93-101.

Cook, M.B., Bhamra, T.A., and Lemon, M., 2006. The transfer and application of product service systems: from academia to UK manufacturing firms. Journal of Cleaner Production, 14(17), 1455-1465.

Davies, A., 2004. Moving base into high-value integrated solutions: a value stream approach. Industrial and Corporate Change, 13(5), 727-756.

Davies, A., and Brady, T., 1998. Policies for a complex product system. Futures, 30(4), 293-304.

Davies, A., and Brady, T., 2000. Organisational capabilities and learning in complex product systems: towards repeatable solutions. Research Policy, 29(7-8), 931-953.

Davies, A., Brady, T., and Hobday, M., 2006. Charting a path toward integrated solutions. MIT Sloan Management Review, 47(3), 39-48.

Davies, A., Brady, T., and Hobday, M., 2007. Organizing for solutions: systems seller vs. systems integrator. Industrial Marketing Management, 36(2), 183-193.

Davis, S.M., 1987. Future perfect. Reading, USA: Addison-Wesley Publishing.

Dobers, P., and Wolff, R., 1999. Eco-efficiency and dematerialization: scenarios for new industrial logics in recycling industries, automobile and household appliances. Business Strategy & the Environment, 8(1), 31-45.

Docters, R., Schefers, B., Durman, C., and Gieskes, M., 2006. Bundles with sharp teeth: effective product combinations. Journal of Business Strategy, 27(5), 10-16.

Doster, D., and Roegner, E., 2005. Setting the pace with solutions. Marketing Management, 9(Spring), 51-54.

Duray, R., Ward, P.T., Milligan, G.W., and Berry, W.L., 2000. Approaches to mass customization: configurations and empirical validation. Journal of Operations Management, 18(6), 605-625.

Economist 2008, Jan 08. Rolls-Royce - Britain's lonely high-flier. Retrieved February 23, 2012, from http://www.economist.com/node/12887368

Eggert, A., and Wolfgang U., 2002. Customer perceived value: a substitute for satisfaction in business markets? Journal of Business & Industrial Marketing, 17(2/3), 107-118.

Eisenhardt, K.M., 1989. Building theories from case study research. Academy of Management Review, 14(4), 532-550.

Evans, S., Partidário, P.J., and Lambert, J., 2007. Industrialization as a key element of sustainable product-service solutions. International Journal of Production Research, 45(18-19), 4225-4246.

Fang, E., Palmatier, R.W., and Steenkamp, J.-B.E.M., 2008. Effect of service transition strategies on firm value. Journal of Marketing, 72(5), 1-14.

Fischer, T., Gebauer, H., Gregory, M., Ren, G., and Fleisch, E., 2010. Exploitation or exploration in service business development? Insights from a dynamic capabilities perspective. Journal of Service Management, 21(5), 591-624.

Flath, D., 1980. The economics of short-term leasing. Economic Inquiry, 18(2), 247-259.

Flowers, S., 2004. Contingent capabilities and the procurement of complex product systems. International Journal of Innovation Management, 8(1), 1-20.

Foote, N.W., Galbraith, J., Hope, Q., and Miller, D., 2001. Making solutions the answer. McKinsey Quarterly, 3, 84-93.

Frambach, R.T., Wels-Lips, I., and Gündlach, A., 1997. Proactive product service strategies: an application in the European health market. Industrial Marketing Management, 26(4), 341-352.

Franke, N., and Piller, F.T., 2003. Key research issues in user interaction with user toolkits in a mass customisation system. International Journal of Technology Management, 26(5/6), 578-599.

Füller, J., Bartl, M., Ernst, H., and Mühlbacher, H., 2006. Community based innovation: how to integrate members of virtual communities into new product development. Electronic Commerce Research, 6(1), 57-73.

Gadiesh, O., and Gilbert, J.L., 1998. Profit pools: a fresh look at strategy. Harvard Business Review, 76(3), 139-47.

Galbraith, J.R., 2002. Organizing to deliver solutions. Organizational Dynamics, 31(2), 194-207.

Gann, D.M., 2000. Innovation in project-based, service-enhanced firms: the construction of complex products and systems. Research Policy, 29(7-8), 955-972.

Gardner, D.J., 2009. Mass customization: an enterprise-wide business strategy. Cupertino, USA: Happy About.

Gebauer, H., 2007. An investigation of antecedents for the development of customer support services in manufacturing companies. Journal of Business-to-Business Marketing, 14(3), 59-96.

Gebauer, H., and Friedli, T., 2005. Behavioral implications of the transition process from products to services. Journal of Business & Industrial Marketing, 20(2), 70-78.

Gebauer, H., Bravo-Sanchez, C., and Fleisch, E., 2008. Service strategies in product manufacturing companies. Business Strategy Series, 9(1), 12-20.

Gebauer, H., Edvardsson, B., Gustafsson, A., and Witell, L., 2010. Match or mismatch: strategy-structure configurations in the service business of manufacturing companies. Journal of Service Research, 13(2), 198-215.

Gebauer, H., Fleisch, E., and Friedli, T., 2005. Overcoming the service paradox in manufacturing companies. European Management Journal, 23(1), 14-26.

Gebauer, H., Friedli, T., and Fleisch, E., 2006. Success factors for achieving high service revenues in manufacturing companies. Benchmarking: An International Journal, 13(3), 374-386.

Gebauer, H., Krempl, R., and Fleisch, E., 2008. Exploring the effect of cognitive biases on customer support services. Creativity & Innovation Management, 17(1), 58-70.

Gebauer, H., Krempl, R., Fleisch, E., and Friedli, T., 2008. Innovation of product-related services. Managing Service Quality, 18(4), 387-404.

Gebauer, H., Paiola, M., and Edvardsson, B., 2010. Service business development in small and medium capital goods manufacturing companies. Managing Service Quality, 20(2), 123-139.

Gilham, I., and Rowland, T., 2001. Predictive medicine: potential benefits from the integration of diagnostics and pharmaceuticals. International Journal of Medical Marketing, 2(1), 18-22.

Gilmore, J.H., and Pine, B.J., 1997. The four faces of customization. Harvard Business Review, 75(1), 91-101.

Glaser, B.G., and Strauss, A.L., 1967. The discovery of grounded theory: strategies for qualitative research. Chicago, USA: Aldine.

Goedkoop, M.J., van Halen, C.J.G., te Riele, H.R.M., and Rommens, P.J.M, 1999. Product service systems: ecological and economic basics. Report for Dutch Ministries of Environment (VROM) and Economic Affairs (EZ).

Goh, Y., and McMahon, C., 2009. Improving reuse of in-service information capture and feedback. Journal of Manufacturing Technology Management, 20(5), 626-639.

Goldman, S.L., Nagel, R.N., and Preiss, K., 1994. Agile competitors and virtual organizations: strategies for enriching the customer. New York, USA: Wiley.

Gordon, M.J., 1974. A general solution to the buy or lease decision: a pedagogical note. Journal of Finance, 29(1), 245-250.

Grenadier, S.R., 1995. Valuing lease contracts - a real-options approach. Journal of Financial Economics, 38(3), 297-331.

Grönroos, C., 2000. Service management and marketing. A customer relationship management approach, Chichester, UK: Wiley.

Grönroos, C., and Helle, P., 2010. Adopting a service logic in manufacturing: conceptual foundation and metrics for mutual value creation. Journal of Service Management, 21(5), 564-590.

Halme, M., Anttonen, M., Hrauda, G., and Kortman, J., 2006. Sustainability evaluation of European household services. Journal of Cleaner Production, 14(17), 1529-1540.

Halme, M., Jasch, C., and Scharp, M., 2004. Sustainable homeservices? Toward household services that enhance ecological, social and economic sustainability. Ecological Economics, 51(1-2), 125-138.

Hamel, G., 1998. Strategy innovation and the quest for value. Sloan Management Review, 39(2), 7-14.

Hansen, K.L., and Rush, H., 1998. Hotspots in complex product systems: emerging issues in innovation management. Technovation, 18(8/9), 555-561.

Hardstone, G.A.P., 2004. Capabilities, structures and strategies re-examined: incumbent firms and the emergence of complex product systems (CoPS). Technology Analysis & Strategic Management, 16(2), 173-196.

Harrison, W., 2003. Beyond the product. Pathfinders Downunder, Melbourne, Victoria.

Harrison, W., 2004. Beyond the product: value creation strategies. Manufacturers' Monthly, 2004 (May), 22-23.

Hart, C.W., 1996. Made to order. Marketing Management, 5(2), 11-23.

Hartmann, A., and Girmscheid, G., 2004. The innovation potential of integrated services and its utilisation through co-operation. Engineering, Construction and Architectural Management, 11(5), 335-341.

Hax, A.C., and Wilde, D.L.I., 1999. The delta model: adaptive management for a changing world. Sloan Management Review, 40(2), 11-28.

Heskett, J.L., Sasser, W.E., and Schlesinger, L.A., 1997. The service profit chain. New York, USA: Free Press.

Hienerth, C., 2006. The commercialization of user innovations: the development of the rodeo kayak industry. R&D Management, 36(3), 273-294.

Hippel, E., 1986. Lead users: a source of novel product concepts. Management Science, 32(7), 791-805.

Hirschl, B., Konrad, W., and Scholl, G., 2003. New concepts in product use for sustainable consumption. Journal of Cleaner Production, 11, 873-881.

Hobday, M., 1998. Product complexity, innovation and industrial organisation. Research Policy, 26(6), 689-710.

Hobday, M., and Rush, H., 1999. Technology management in complex product systems (CoPS)-ten questions answered. International Journal of Technology Management, 17(6), 618-638.

Hobday, M., Davies, A., and Prencipe, A., 2005. Systems integration: a core capability of the modern corporation. Industrial & Corporate Change, 14(6), 1109-1143.

Holmström, J., Brax, S., and Ala-Risku, T., 2010. Comparing provider-customer constellations of visibility-based service. Journal of Service Management, 21(5), 675-692.

Homburg, C., and Garbe, B., 1999. Towards an improved understanding of industrial services: quality dimensions and their impact on buyer-seller relationships. Journal of Business-to-Business Marketing, 6(2), 39-71.

Homburg, C., Faßnacht, M., and Günther, C., 2002. Erfolgreiche Umsetzung dienstleistungsorientierter Strategien von Industriegüterunternehmen. Zeitschrift für betriebswirtschaftliche Forschung, 54(6), 487-508.

Hornschild, K., Kinkel, S., and Lay, G., 2004. Product-related Services: Operator Models in German Mechanical Engineering Firms. Economic Bulletin, 41(2), 65-68.

Huff, A.S., 2009. Designing research for publication. Thousand Oaks, USA: Sage.

Hypko, P., Tilebein, M., and Gleich, R., 2010a. Clarifying the concept of performance-based contracting in manufacturing industries: a research synthesis. Journal of Service Management, 21(5), 625-655.

Hypko, P., Tilebein, M., and Gleich, R., 2010b. Benefits and uncertainties of performance-based contracting in manufacturing industries: an agency theory perspective. Journal of Service Management, 21(4), 460-489.

Jespersen, J., 1999. Reconciling environment and employment by switching from goods to services? A review of Danish experience. European Environment, 9(1), 17-23.

Johansson, J.E., Krishnamurthy, C., and Schlissberg, H.E., 2003. Solving the solutions problem. McKinsey Quarterly, (3), 116-125.

Johansson, P., and Olhager, J., 2004. Industrial service profiling: matching service offerings and processes. International Journal of Production Economics, 89(3), 309-320.

Johnson, M., and Mena, C., 2008. Supply chain management for servitised products: a multi-industry case study. International Journal of Production Economics, 114(1), 27-39.

Johnstone, S., Dainty, A., and Wilkinson, A., 2008. In search of "product-service": evidence from aerospace, construction, and engineering. Service Industries Journal, 28(6), 861-875.

Johnstone, S., Dainty, A., and Wilkinson, A., 2009. Integrating products and services through life: an aerospace experience. International Journal of Operations & Production Management, 29(5), 520-538.

Kim, W.C., and Mauborgne, R., 1997. Value innovation: the strategic logic of high growth. Harvard Business Review, 75(1), 103-112.

Kim, W.C., and Mauborgne, R., 1999. Strategy, value innovation, and the knowledge economy. Sloan Management Review, 40(3), 41-54.

Kim, W.C., and Mauborgne, R., 2005. Blue ocean strategy: how to create uncontested market space and make competition irrelevant. Boston, USA: Harvard Business School Press.

Kimita, K., Shimomura, Y., and Arai, T., 2009. Evaluation of customer satisfaction for PSS design. Journal of Manufacturing Technology Management, 20(5), 654-673.

Klaus, P., and Maklan, S., 2007. The role of brands in a service-dominated world. Journal of Brand Management, 15, 115-122.

Knecht, T., Leszinski, R., and Weber, F.A., 1993. Memo to a CEO: making profits after the sale. McKinsey Quarterly, 1993(4) pp.79-86.

Korte, S., Rijkers-Defrasne, S., and Zweck, A., 2009. Hybride Wertschöpfung – Internationale Übersichtsstudie. Zukünftige Technologien Consulting VDI Technologiezentrum GmbH, Düsseldorf.

Kotha, S., 1995. Mass customization: implementing the emerging paradigm for competitive advantage. Strategic Management Journal, 16(S1), 21-42.

Kotha, S., 1996. From mass production to mass customization: the case of the national industrial bicycle company of Japan. European Management Journal, 14(5), 442-450.

Kotler, P., 1994. Marketing management: analysis, planning, implementation, and control. Upper Saddle River, USA: Prentice Hall.

Krishnamurthy, C., Johansson, J.E., and Schlissberg, H.E., 2003. Solution selling: is the pain worth the gain? McKinsey Marketing Solutions, McKinsey & Co.

Krucken, L., and Meroni, A., 2006. Building stakeholder networks to develop and deliver product-service-systems: practical experiences on elaborating pro-active materials for communication. Journal of Cleaner Production, 14(17), 1502-1508.

Lampel, J., and Mintzberg, H., 1996. Customizing customization. Sloan Management Review, 38(1), 21-30.

Lay, G., Copani, G., Jäger, A., and Biege, S., 2010. The relevance of service in European manufacturing industries. Journal of Service Management, 21(5), 715-726.

Leimeister, J.M., Knebel, U., and Krcmar, H., 2010. Hybrid value creation in the sports industry: the case of a mobile sports companion as IT-supported product-service-bundle. International Journal of Information Systems in the Service Sector, 2(1), 11-25.

Leiringer, R., Green, S.D., and Raja, J.Z., 2009. Living up to the value agenda: the empirical realities of through-life value creation in construction. Construction Management and Economics, 27(3), 271-285.

Lele, M.M., 1997. After-sales service - necessary evil or strategic opportunity? Managing Service Quality, 7(3), 141-145.

Lenfle, S., and Midler, C., 2009. The launch of innovative product-related services: lessons from automotive telematics. Research Policy, 38(1), 159-169.

Lepak, D.P., Smith, K.G., and Taylor, S.M., 2007. Value creation and value capture: a multilevel perspective. Academy of Management Review, 32(1), 180-194.

Lettl, C., Herstatt, C., and Gemuenden H.G., 2006. Users' contributions to radical innovation: evidence from four cases in the field of medical equipment technology. R&D Management, 36 (3), 251-272.

Levitt, T., 1980. Marketing success through differentiation - of anything. Harvard Business Review, 58(1), 83-91.

Lewellen, W.G., Long, M.S., and McConnell, J.J., 1976. Asset leasing in competitive capital markets. The Journal of Finance, XXXI(3), 787-798.

Lüthje, C., and Herstatt, C., 2004. The lead user method: an outline of empirical findings and issues for future research. R&D Management, 34(5), 553-568.

MacMillan, I.C., and McGrath, R.G., 1997. Discovering new points of differentiation. Harvard Business Review, 75(July-August), 133-8, 143-5.

Magnusson, T., Tell, F., and Watson, J., 2005. From CoPS to mass production? Capabilities and innovation in power generation equipment manufacturing. Industrial and Corporate Change, 14(1), 1-26.

Malleret, V., 2006. Value creation through service offers. European Management Journal, 24(1), 106-116.

Maloney, W.F., 2002. Construction product/service and customer satisfaction. Journal of construction engineering and management, 128(6), 522-529.

Manzini, E., and Vezzoli, C., 2002. Product-service systems and sustainability: opportunities for sustainable solutions. Report, United Nations Environment Programme (UNEP), Division of Technology Industry and Economics.

Markides, C., 1997. Strategic innovation. Sloan Management Review, 38(3), 9-23.

Martin (Jr), C.R., and Horne, D.A., 1992. Restructuring towards a service orientation: the strategic challenges. International Journal of Service Industry Management, 3(1), 25-38.

Mathieu, V., 2001a. Product services: from a service supporting the product to a service supporting the client. Journal of Business & Industrial Marketing, 16(1), 39-61.

Mathieu, V., 2001b. Service strategies within the manufacturing sector: benefits, costs and partnership. International Journal of Service Industry Management, 12(5), 451-475.

Matthyssens, P., and Vandenbempt, K., 2008. Moving from basic offerings to value-added solutions: Strategies, barriers and alignment. Industrial Marketing Management, 37(3), 316-328.

Matthyssens, P., and Vandenbempt, K., 2010. Service addition as business market strategy: identification of transition trajectories. Journal of Service Management, 21(5), 693-714.

Maxwell, D., and van der Vorst, R., 2003. Developing sustainable products and services. Journal of Cleaner Production, 11(8), 883-895.

Maxwell, D., Sheate, W., and van der Vorst, R., 2006. Functional and systems aspects of the sustainable product and service development approach for industry. Journal of Cleaner Production, 14(17), 1466-1479.

McNeill, R.B., 1944. The lease as a marketing tool. Harvard Business Review, 22(summer), 415-430.

Meijkamp, R., 1998. Changing consumer behaviour through eco-efficient services: an empirical study of car sharing in the Netherlands. Business Strategy and the Environment, 7(4), 234-244.

Miles, M.B., and Huberman, A.M., 1994. Qualitative data analysis: an expanded sourcebook ET. 2nd edition, Thousand Oaks, USA: Sage.

Miller, D., Hope, Q., Eisenstat, R., Foote, N.W., and Galbraith, J., 2002. The problem of solutions: balancing clients and capabilities. Business Horizons, 45(2), 3-12.

Miller, M.H., and Upton, C.W., 1976. Leasing, buying, and the cost of capital services. The Journal of Finance, XXXI(3), 761-786.

Miller, R., Hobday, M., Leroux-Demers, T., and Olleros, X., 1995. Innovation in complex systems industries: the case of flight simulation. Industrial and Corporate Change, 4(2), 363-400.

Molloy, E., Siemieniuch, C., and Sinclair, M., 2009. Decision-making systems and the product-to-service shift. Journal of Manufacturing Technology Management, 20(5), 606-625.

Mont, O., 2002a. Clarifying the concept of product-service system. Journal of Cleaner Production, 10(3), 237-245.

Mont, O., 2002b. Drivers and barriers for shifting towards more service-oriented businesses: analysis of the PSS field and contributions from Sweden. The Journal of Sustainable Product Design, 2(3-4), 89-103.

Mont, O., 2004a. Institutionalisation of sustainable consumption patterns based on shared use. Ecological Economics, 50(1-2), 135-153.

Mont, O., 2004b. Product-service systems: panacea or myth? Dissertation, The International Institute for Industrial Environmental Economics (IIIEE), Lund University, Lund, Sweden.

Mont, O., 2004c. Reducing life-cycle environmental impacts through systems of joint use. Greener Management International, 45(Spring), 63-77.

Mont, O., and Lindhqvist, T., 2003. The role of public policy in advancement of product service systems. Journal of Cleaner Production, 11(8), 905-914.

Mont, O., Dalhammar, C., and Jacobsson, N., 2006. A new business model for baby prams based on leasing and product remanufacturing. Journal of Cleaner Production, 14(17), 1509-1518.

More, R., 2001. Creating profits from integrated product-service strategies. Ivey Business Journal, 65(5), 75-81.

Morelli, N, 2003. Product-service systems, a perspective shift for designers: a case study - the design of a telecentre. Design Studies, 24, 73-99.

Morelli, N., 2002. Designing product/service systems: a methodological exploration. Design Issues, 18(3), 3-17.

Morelli, N., 2006. Developing new product service systems (PSS): methodologies and operational tools. Journal of Cleaner Production, 14(17), 1495-1501.

Morelli, N., 2009. Service as value co-production: reframing the service design process. Journal of Manufacturing Technology Management, 20(5), 568-590.

Möslein, K.M., 2005. Der Markt für Managementwissen. Wiesbaden, Germany: Gabler.

Möslein, K.M., Adamczyk, S., and Velamuri, V.K., 2010. Wertschaffende Eigenschaften und Kategorien hybrider Wertschöpfung. In Leimeister, J.M., Krcmar, H., Halle, M., and Möslein, K.M., eds. Hybride Wertschöpfung in der Gesundheitsförderung. Innovation - Dienstleistung - IT. Lohmar, Germany: Eul, 19-44.

Möslein, K.M., and Kölling, M., 2007. Interaktive hybride Wertschöpfung als Innovationsstrategie. In Streich, D., and Wahl, D., eds. Innovationsfähigkeit in einer modernen Arbeitswelt. Frankfurt, Germany: Campus, 195-202.

Möslein, K.M., and Velamuri, V.K., 2009. Hybrid value creation as innovation strategy. In Fisch, J.H., and Roß, J.M., eds. Fallstudien zum Innovationsmanagement. Wiesbaden, Germany: Gabler, 485-500.

Moultrie, J., Clarkson, P.J., and Probert, D.R., 2006. Development of a product audit tool. Proceedings of the Institution of Mechanical Engineers, Part B: Journal of Engineering Manufacture, 220(7), 1157-1174.

Neely, A., 2008. Exploring the financial consequences of the servitization of manufacturing. Operations Management Research, 1(2), 103-118.

Neu, W.A., and Brown, S.W., 2008. Manufacturers forming successful complex business services: designing an organization to fit the market. International Journal of Service Industry Management, 19(2), 232-251.

Neu, W.A., and Brown, S.W., 2005. Forming successful business-to-business services in goods-dominant firms. Journal of Service Research, 8(1), 3.

Ng, I.C.L., and Nudurupati, S.S., 2010. Outcome-based service contracts in the defence industry - mitigating the challenges. Journal of Service Management, 21(5), 656-674.

Nordin, F., and Kowalkowski, C., 2010. Solutions offerings: a critical review and reconceptualisation. Journal of Service Management, 21(4), 441-459.

Obenberger, R.W., and Brown, S.W., 1976. A marketing alternative: consumer leasing and renting. Business Horizons, 19(5), 82-86.

Oliva, R., and Kallenberg, R., 2003. Managing the transition from products to services. International Journal of Service Industry Management, 14(2), 160-172.

Page, A.L., and Siemplenski, M., 1983. Product systems marketing. Industrial Marketing Management, 12(2), 89-99.

Paoli, M., and Prencipe, A., 1999. The role of knowledge bases in complex product systems: some empirical evidence from the aero engine industry. Journal of Management and Governance, 3(2), 137-160.

Pawar, K.S., Beltagui, A., and Riedel, J.C.K.H., 2009. The PSO triangle: designing product, service and organisation to create value. International Journal of Operations & Production Management, 29(5), 468-493.

Penttinen, E., and Palmer, J., 2007. Improving firm positioning through enhanced offerings and buyer-seller relationships. Industrial Marketing Management, 36(5), 552-564.

Phillips, F., Ochs, L., and Schrock, M., 1999. The product is dead - long live the product-service! Research Technology Management, 42(4), 51-56.

Piller, F., 2006. Mass Customization: Ein wettbewerbsstrategisches Konzept im Informationszeitalter. Wiesbaden, Germany: Gabler.

Piller, F.T., and Franke, N., 2004. Value creation by toolkits for user innovation and design: the case of the watch market. The Journal of Product Innovation Management, 21, 401-415.

Piller, F.T., and Tseng, M.M., 2010. Handbook of research in mass customization and personalization. Singapore: World Scientific Publishing Company.

Piller, F.T., and Walcher, D., 2006. Toolkits for idea competitions: a novel method to integrate users in new product development. R&D Management, 36(3), 307-318.

Piller, F.T., Möslein, K.M and Stotko, C.M., 2004. Does mass customization pay? An economic approach to evaluate customer integration. Product Planning and Control, 15(4), 435-444.

Pine, B.J., 1992. Mass Customization: the new frontier in business competition. Boston, USA: Harvard Business School Press.

Pine, B.J., Victor, B., and Boynton, A.C., 1993. Making mass customization work. Harvard Business Review, 108-119.

Pittaway, L., Robertson, M., Munir, K., Denyer, D and Neely, A., 2004. Networking and innovation: a systematic review of the evidence. International Journal of Management Reviews, 5-6(3-4), 137-168.

Porter, M.E., 1998. Competitive Strategy: Techniques for analyzing industries and competitors. New York, USA: Free Press.

Potts, G.W., 1988. Exploit your product's service life cycle. Harvard Business Review, 66(5), 32-36.

Prencipe, A., 1998. Modular design and complex product systems: facts, promises, and questions. CoPS Publication No. 47, Complex Product Systems Innovation Centre, Freeman Centre, University of Sussex, UK.

Prettenthaler, F.E., and Steininger, K.W., 1999. From ownership to service use lifestyle: the potential of car sharing. Ecological Economics, 28(3), 443-453.

Prügl, R., and Schreier, M., 2006. Learning from leading-edge customers at The Sims: opening up the innovation process using toolkits. R&D Management, 36(3), 237-250

Quinn, J.B., Doorley, T.L., and Paquette, P.C., 1990. Beyond products: services-based strategy. Harvard Business Review, 68(2), 58-67.

Raddats, C., and Easingwood, C., 2010. Services growth options for B2B product-centric businesses. Industrial Marketing Management, 39(8), 1334-1345.

Reichwald, R., and Piller, F.T., 2009. Interaktive Wertschöpfung: Open Innovation, Individualisierung und neue Formen der Arbeitsteilung. 2nd edition, Wiesbaden, Germany: Gabler.

Rese, M., Strotmann, W., and Karger, M., 2009. Which industrial product service system fits best? Journal of Manufacturing Technology Management, 20(5), 640-653.

Rexfelt, O., and Hiort af Ornäs, V., 2009. Consumer acceptance of product-service systems: designing for relative advantages and uncertainty reductions. Journal of Manufacturing Technology Management, 20(5), 674-699.

Riemer, K., and Totz, C., 2003. The many faces of personalization - an integrative overview of mass customization and personalization. In Tseng, M.M., and Piller F.T., eds. The customer centric enterprise: advances in mass customization and personalization. Berlin, Germany: Springer, 35-50

Robinson, T., Clarke-Hill, C.M., and Clarkson, R., 2002. Differentiation through service: a perspective from the commodity chemicals sector. Service Industries Journal, 22(3), 149-166.

Rocchi, S., 2005. Enhancing sustainable innovation by design. An approach to the co-creation of economic, social and environmental value. Dissertation, Erasmus University, Rotterdam, Netherlands.

Roegner, E.V., Seifert, T., and Swinford, D.D., 2001. Putting a price on solutions. The McKinsey Quarterly, (3), 94-98.

Roy, R., 2000. Sustainable product-service systems. Futures, 32(3), 289-299.

Rush, H., Hobday, M., and Tidd, J., 2000. Innovation in complex products and system. Research Policy, 29(7-8), 793-804.

Samli, A.C., Jacobs, L.W., and Wills, J., 1992. What presale and postsale services do you need to be competitive. Industrial Marketing Management, 21, 33-41.

Sawhney, M., 2006. Going beyond the product: defining, designing and delivering customer solutions. In Lusch, R.F., and Vargo, S.L., eds. The service dominant logic of marketing: dialogue, debate and directions. New York, USA: M.E. Sharpe, 365-380.

Sawhney, M., Balasubramanian, S., and Krishnan, V.V., 2004. Creating growth with services. MIT Sloan Management Review, (Winter), 34-43.

Schenk, M., Ryll, F., and Schady, R., 2006. Anforderungen an den Produktentwicklungsprozess für hybride Produkte im Anlagenbau. Industrie Management, 22(1), 55-58.

Schmenner, R.W., 2009. Manufacturing, service, and their integration: some history and theory. International Journal of Operations & Production Management, 29(5), 431-443.

Schmitz, G., 2008. Der wahrgenommene Wert hybrider Produkte: Konzeptionelle Grundlagen und Komponenten. Paper presented at Multikonferenz Wirtschaftsinformatik (MKWI), Berlin, Germany, February 26-28, 2008.

Schuh, G., Lenders, M., Bartoschek, M., and Bender, D., 2008. Preisfindungsprozess für Leistungssysteme im Maschinen- und Anlagenbau. Controlling, 20(8-9), 481-487.

Sharma, A., Iyer, G., and Evanschitzky, H., 2008. Personal selling of high-technology products: the solution-selling imperative. Journal of Relationship Marketing, 7(3), 287-308.

Sharma, D., and Molloy, R., 1999. The truth about customer solutions. Viewpoint, Booz Allen & Hamilton.

Shepherd, C., and Ahmed, P.K., 2000. From product innovation to solutions innovation: a new paradigm for competitive advantage. European Journal of Innovation Management, 3(2), 100-106.

Sievänen, M., 2004. The effects of customization on capital goods manufacturing business. Dissertation, Tampere University of Technology, Tampere, Finland.

Silveira, G.D., Borenstein, D., and Fogliatto, F.S., 2001. Mass customization: literature review and research directions. International Journal of Production Economics, 72, 1-13.

Slywotzky, A., and Wise, R., 2003. Demand innovation: GM's OnStar case. Strategy & Leadership, 31(4), 17-22.

Stille, F., 2003. Product related services - still growing in importance. Economic Bulletin, 40, 195-200.

Stremersch, S., and Tellis, G.J., 2002. Strategic bundling of products and prices: a new synthesis for marketing. Journal of Marketing, 66(1), 55-72.

Stremersch, S., Wuyts, S., and Frambach, R.T., 2001. The purchasing of full-service contracts: an exploratory study within the industrial maintenance market. Industrial Marketing Management, 30(1), 1-12.

Sturm, F., and Bading, A., 2008. Investitionsgüterhersteller als Anbieter industrieller Lösungen - Bestandsaufnahme des Wandels anhand einer Umfrage. Wirtschaftsinformatik, 50(3), 174-186.

Sundin, E., Lindahl, M., and Ijomah, W., 2009. Product design for product/service systems: design experiences from Swedish industry. Journal of Manufacturing Technology Management, 20(5), 723-753.

Tanner, J.F., 1996. Buyer perceptions of the purchase process and its effect on customer satisfaction. Industrial Marketing Management, 25(2), 125-133.

Tasaki, T., Hashimoto, S., and Moriguchi, Y., 2006. A quantitative method to evaluate the level of material use in lease/reuse systems of electrical and electronic equipment. Journal of Cleaner Production, 14(17), 1519-1528.

Teece, D.J., 2009. Business models, business strategy and innovation. Long range planning, 43(2), 172-194

Thomas, O., and Nüttgens, M., 2009. Dienstleistungsmodellierung: Methoden, Werkzeuge und Branchenlösungen. Berlin, Germany: Physica-Verlag.

Thomas, O., Walter, P., and Loos, P., 2008. Product-Service Systems: Konstruktion und Anwendung einer Entwicklungsmethodik. Wirtschaftsinformatik, 50(3), 208-219.

Tranfield, D., Denyer, D., and Smart, P., 2003. Towards a methodology for developing evidence-informed management knowledge by means of systematic review. British Journal of Management, 14(3), 207-222.

Tucker, R.B., 2001. Strategy innovation takes imagination. Journal of Business Strategy, 22(3), 23-27.

Tukker, A., 2004. Eight types of product-service system: eight ways to sustainability? Experiences from SusProNet. Business Strategy and the Environment, 13(4), 246-260.

Tuli, K.R., Kohli, A.K., and Bharadwaj, S.G., 2007. Rethinking customer solutions: from product bundles to relational processes. Journal of Marketing, 71(3), 1-17.

Vandermerwe, S., 2000. How increasing value to customers improves business results. Sloan Management Review, 42(1), 27-37.

Vandermerwe, S., and Rada, J., 1988. Servitization of business: adding value by adding services. European Management Journal, 6(4), 314-324.

Vargo, S.L., and Lusch, R.F., 2004. Evolving to a new dominant logic for marketing. Journal of Marketing, 68(1), 1-17.

Vargo, S.L., and Lusch, R.F., 2006. Service-dominant logic - what it is, what it is not, what it might be. In Lusch, R.F., and Vargo, S.L., eds. The service dominant logic of marketing: dialogue, debate and directions. New York, USA: M.E. Sharpe, 43-56.

Varian, H.R., 2000. Buying, sharing and renting of information goods. The Journal of Industrial Economics, XLVIII(4), 473-488.

Velamuri, V.K., Bansemir, B., Neyer, A.-K., and Möslein, K.M., 2013. Product service systems as a driver for business model innovation: Lessons learned from the manufacturing industry. International Journal of Innovation Management, 17(1), (forthcoming).

Velamuri, V.K., Neyer, A.-K., and Möslein, K.M., 2008. What influences the design of hybrid products? Lessons learned from the preventive health-care industry. Paper presented at the 15th International Product Development Management Conference (IPDMC), Hamburg, June 29- July 1, 2008.

Velamuri, V.K., Neyer, A.-K., and Möslein, K.M., 2010. Hybrid value creation: understanding the value creating attributes. In Böhmann, T., and Leimeister, J.M., eds. Integration von Produkt & Dienstleistung - Hybride Wertschöpfung. Norderstedt, Germany: Books on Demand, 3-16.

Velamuri, V.K., Neyer, A.-K., and Möslein, K.M., 2011. Hybrid value creation: a systematic review of an evolving research area. Journal für Betriebswirtschaft, 61(1), 3-35.

Ward, Y., and Graves, A., 2007. Through-life management: the provision of total customer solutions in the aerospace industry. International Journal of Services Technology & Management, 8(6), 455-477.

Webster (Jr), F.E., 1992. The changing role of marketing in the corporation. The Journal of Marketing, 56(4), 1-17.

Williams, A., 2006. Product-Service Systems in the automotive industry: the case of micro-factory retailing. Journal of Cleaner Production, 14(2), 172-184.

Windahl, C., and Lakemond, N., 2006. Developing integrated solutions: the importance of relationships within the network. Industrial Marketing Management, 35(7), 806-818.

Windahl, C., and Lakemond, N., 2010. Integrated solutions from a service-centered perspective: Applicability and limitations in the capital goods industry. Industrial Marketing Management, 39(8), 1278-1290.

Windahl, C., Andersson, P., Berggren, C., and Nehler, C., 2004. Manufacturing firms and integrated solutions: characteristics and implications. European Journal of Innovation Management, 7(3), 218-228.

Wise, R., and Baumgartner, P., 1999. Go downstream the new profit imperative in manufacturing. Harvard Business Review, 77(5), 133-141.

Wu, L., Yue, X., and Sim, T., 2006. Supply clusters: a key to China's. Supply Chain Management Review, 10(2), 46-51.

Yin, R.K., 2003. Case study research: design and methods. 3rd ed., Thousand Oaks: Sage.

Zaring, O. (ed.), Bartolomeo, M., Eder, P., Hopkinson, P., Groenewegen, P., James, P., de Jong, P., Nijhuis, L., Scholl, G., Slob, A., and Örninge, M., 2001. Creating eco-efficient producer services. Research Report, Gothenburg Research Institute, Gothenburg, Sweden.

Zellner, G., 2008. Gestaltung hybrider Wertschöpfung mittels Architekturen – Analyse am Beispiel des Business Engineering. Wirtschaftsinformatik, 50(3), 187-195.

# Annexes

# Annex A: Technical Document: www.hybridvaluecreation.com

## 1. Introduction

This technical document describes the website www.hybridvaluecreation.com and the case vignette database that is embedded in the website. In addition to this introduction, where the purpose and target audience is defined, this document consists of four sections:

1. the background: provides an overview of BMBF funded project SPRINT (Systematisches Design zur Integration von Produkt und Dienstleistung in der Gesundheitswirtschaft), FKZ 01FD0610,
2. the website description: provides an overview of the website and its contents,
3. the database: provides an overview of how the database is structured, and
4. the case vignette structure: provides an overview of the structure of individual cases.

The document describes the contents of the website www.hybridvaluecreation.com. This document should be the main guideline when using the website and especially the database consisting of over 100 hybrid value creation case vignettes. The intended reader can be either a researcher or a practitioner in the field of hybrid value creation. The website contains information that is relevant to both types of target audience.

## 2 Background

A paradigm shift can be seen as more and more firms are moving from offering standalone products or services to offering integrated solutions consisting of products and services. The boundary between products and services is constantly being challenged; leading to hybrid value structures. Hybrid products are characterized by the seamless integration of products and services leading to a thoroughly engineered product. Here the product and service aspects cannot be easily separated from each other. This paradigm shift forms the basis for the BMBF's research focus "Integration of products and services".

As part of this research focus, BMBF funded the project SPRINT to deal with the integration of products and services in the context of preventive health care. The project was managed by "Projektträger im Deutschen Zentrum für Luft- und Raumfahrt" (PT-DLR, Project Management Agency - part of the German Aerospace Center). *Figure 17* presents the logos of project Sprint, BMBF and DLR. *Table 33* provides an overview of the project partners.

*Figure 17: Logos of Project SPRINT, BMBF and DLR*

*Table 33: Overview of SPRINT project partners*

| Chair or Center | Description |
|---|---|
| www.winfobase.de | The Chair for Information Systems (WINFO), headed by Prof. Dr. Helmut Krcmar, focuses on the design of IT-based user innovations that are socially acceptable, technologically stable and economically sustainable. |
| www.sport.med.tum.de | The Chair for Prevention and Sports Medicine, headed by Prof. Dr. med. Martin Halle, focuses on research and teaching dealing with sports medicine, preventive medicine and rehabilitation. |
| www.clicresearch.de | The Center for Leading Innovation and Cooperation (CLIC) at the HHL - Leipzig Graduate School of Management, headed by Prof. Dr. Kathrin Möslein, focuses on research dealing with principles, practices and processes that foster the strategic ability of organizations to innovate and inspire people in organizations to build the bridges critical to innovation and value creation. |
| www.cdtm.de | The Center for Digital Technology and Management (CDTM), a joint institution by the Ludwig Maximilian University (LMU) in Munich and the Technische Universität München (TUM). CDTM's research focuses around tele-communication, information technology, media & entertainment, while setting a focus on applied output and prototype development. |

## 3 Website: www.hybridvaluecreation.com

The competence center hybrid value creation is available under www.hybridvaluecreation.com. The website includes an introduction to the phenomenon of hybrid value creation and explains the importance and relevance of it for companies. Furthermore, it includes the case vignette database, which deals with cases of hybrid value creation from different industry sectors. This database includes more than 100 case vignettes and forms the core of the website. In addition, the website provides an overview of research strands dealing with hybrid value creation. *Figures18* and *19* contain screenshots of two pages of the website.

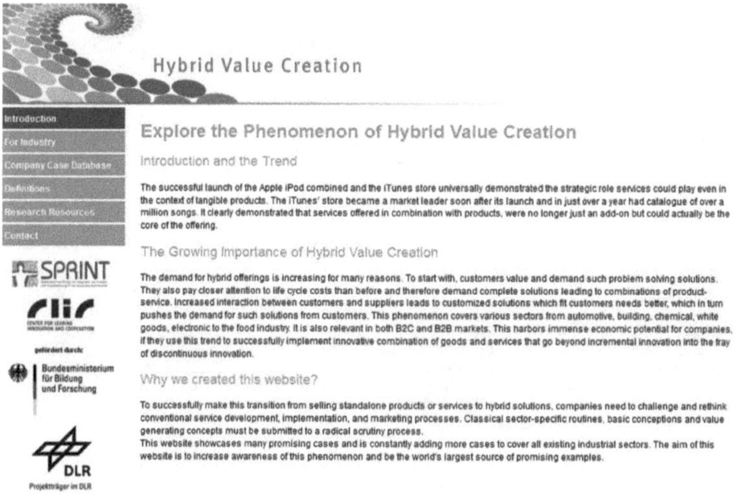


*Figure 18: Screenshots of launch page of website www.hybridvaluecreation.com*

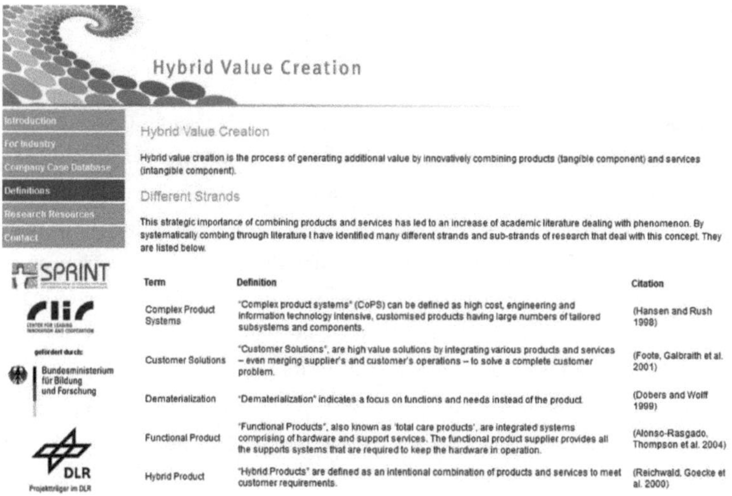

*Figure 19: Screenshots of definitions*

# 4 Database

The database offers a wide range of case studies dealing with hybrid value creation. Everyone (researchers and practitioners) has free access to the database. Small and medium sized enterprises (SMEs) interested in hybrid value creation are encouraged to make use of the database. A screenshot of the database is captured in *Figure 20.*

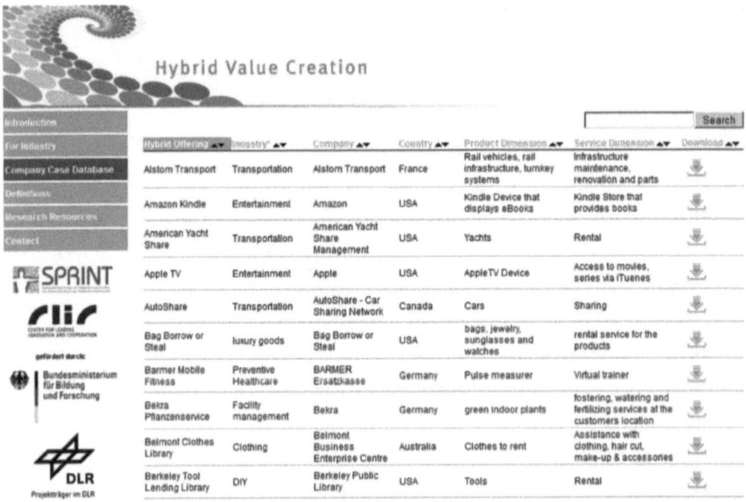


| Hybrid Offering | Industry | Company | Country | Product Dimension | Service Dimension | Download |
|---|---|---|---|---|---|---|
| Alstom Transport | Transportation | Alstom Transport | France | Rail vehicles, rail infrastructure, turnkey systems | Infrastructure maintenance, renovation and parts | |
| Amazon Kindle | Entertainment | Amazon | USA | Kindle Device that displays eBooks | Kindle Store that provides books | |
| American Yacht Share | Transportation | American Yacht Share Management | USA | Yachts | Rental | |
| Apple TV | Entertainment | Apple | USA | AppleTV Device | Access to movies, series via iTuenes | |
| AutoShare | Transportation | AutoShare - Car Sharing Network | Canada | Cars | Sharing | |
| Bag Borrow or Steal | luxury goods | Bag Borrow or Steal | USA | bags, jewelry, sunglasses and watches | rental service for the products | |
| Barmer Mobile Fitness | Preventive Healthcare | BARMER Ersatzkasse | Germany | Pulse measurer | Virtual trainer | |
| Bekra Pflanzenservice | Facility management | Bekra | Germany | green indoor plants | fostering, watering and fertilizing services at the customers location | |
| Belmont Clothes Library | Clothing | Belmont Business Enterprise Centre | Australia | Clothes to rent | Assistance with clothing, hair cut, make-up & accessories | |
| Berkeley Tool Lending Library | DIY | Berkeley Public Library | USA | Tools | Rental | |

*Figure 20: Screenshot of database*

The database is embedded as a table that can be sorted and filtered based on selected criteria. The six main criteria for filtering are: (1) *hybrid offering:* contains the name of the offering, (2) *industry:* states the industry the offerings belongs to, (3) *company:* states the name of the company, (4) *country:* states the county to which the company belongs to, (5) *product dimension:* states the product dimension of each offering, and (6) *service dimension:* states the service dimension of each offering. An icon under downloads signals if a case vignette with additional information is available for download (explained in the next section).

*Figure 21* displays the technical structure of the database (relationship between the six criteria described above). Each hybrid offering has a product and a service dimension. Moreover, each hybrid offering can come from only one company, country and industry. On the other hand, a company, country and industry can have more than one hybrid offering. A company can only come from one country, but a country may have more than one company. Finally, a country and industry have a n:n relationship between each other.

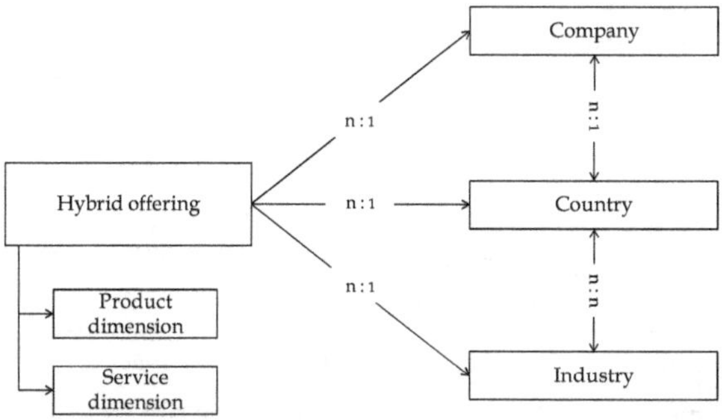


*Figure 21: Technical structure of database*

A search function allows the user to identify cases based on search terms. For e.g., the user can search for "preventive healthcare" and come up with a list of relevant cases (*Figure 22* contains a screenshot of this search function using 'preventive healthcare').

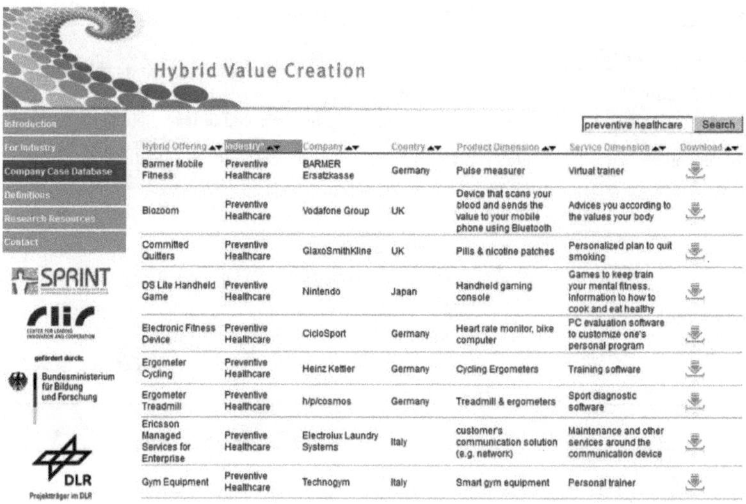

*Figure 22: Screenshot of search result for "preventive healthcare"*

# 5 Case Vignette Structure

For many case vignettes there is an extended version that can be downloaded in PDF format (see *Table 34* for an overview).

*Table 34: Overview of case structure of extended version*

| | |
|---|---|
| **Hybrid offering** | |
| Brief description | A brief description on the offering is provided |
| Hybrid offering's industry | States the industry to which the offerings belong to<br>(e.g. automation, preventive healthcare) |
| **Company details** | |
| Company description | A Brief description of the company is provided |
| Company's industry | States the company's core industry<br>(e.g. chemicals, engineering, pharmaceutical) |
| Country of origin | States the country of origin for the company<br>(e.g. Austria, Germany, Spain) |
| **Dimensions** | |
| Product dimension | A brief description of the product aspect of the offering is provided |
| Service dimension | A brief description of the service aspect of the offering is provided |
| Other links | Provides useful links for further analysis<br>(e.g. company website links or other publications or blogs) |
| **Other Crucial Dimensions** | |
| Hybrid orientation | Sates the focus of the hybrid offering<br>(e.g. product oriented, service oriented or use oriented) |
| Community as service | States if the offering includes community functions as a part of the service dimension<br>(e.g. social network, forums etc.) |
| Target market | States the target market of the offering<br>(e.g. business-to-business (b2b) or a business-to-customer (b2c) market or a combination of both) |
| Revenue model | States the identified revenue model<br>(e.g. upfront payment, monthly rental, pay per use, fixed price contracts) |
| **Images** | |
| Provides images of product and service dimensions (only if available) | |

*Figures* 23 and 24 are two case vignette examples that can be downloaded from the database.

Hybrid Value Creation.com

# miCoach

| Hybrid Offering | |
|---|---|
| **Brief description** | The miCoach system is a joint offering by adidas and Samsung. It is a real-time training system designed to motivate, inspire and enable athletes at all levels to reach their training goals. The whole system comprises of five components: the adidas co-branded miCoach Samsung mobile phone (F110), a heart rate monitor, a stride sensor chip that fits regular running footwear, compatible adidas apparel and the miCoach website that helps one create tailored training programs. |
| **Hybrid offering's industry** | Fitness |
| **Company details** | |
| Adidas Group<br>www.adidas.de/ | adidas is a global designer, developer and marketer of athletic footwear, apparel and accessories. The company was founded in the year 1949 in Herzogenaurach, Germany and is one of the biggest sporting goods companies in the world. The adidas group consists of the three brands adidas, Reebok and Taylor made. |
| **Company's industry** | Sporting goods |
| **Country of origin** | Germany |
| **Dimensions** | |
| **Product dimension** | miCoach consists of several products. It consists of a Samsung mobile phone (F110) with earphones, a heart rate monitor and a stride sensor chip that fits regular running footwear. |
| **Service dimension** | Two services are used in the miCoach system. The first service is software on the mobile phone which gives real-time feedback to the runner. By measuring the heartbeat the system gives the user instant feedback through the attached earphone to make sure that one does not over-exert or under-perform. In addition to that, the software selects music that is most suitable to the current running speed.<br>The other service is the website that is used for storing, reviewing and evaluating the information that was gathered during the runs. |
| **Other links** | |
| **Other Crucial Dimensions** | |
| **Hybrid orientation** | Product Oriented |
| **Community as service** | No |
| **Target market** | B2C |
| **Revenue model** | One time payment at purchase |

**Images**

Product dimension

Service Dimension

Information Systems I - Innovation & Value Creation
Friedrich-Alexander University Erlangen-Nuremberg
Lange Gasse 20, 90403 Nuremberg, Germany
www.wi1.uni-erlangen.de

Vivek K. Velamuri
Tel.: +49 (0)911 5302 152
vivek.velamuri@wiso.uni-erlangen.de
www.hybridvaluecreation.com

*Figure 23: Example of case miCoach*

Hybrid Value Creation.com

# Posh Bags 4 Rent

| | |
|---|---|
| **Hybrid Offering** | |
| **Brief description** | PoshBags4Rent is a company that focuses on the rental of expensive purses and handbags. After the user is registered on the company's homepage, luxury bags from companies such as Luis Vuitton, Aigner, Gucci, Chanel and Dior can be rented for a weekly fee. |
| **Hybrid offering's industry** | Luxury Goods, Handbags |
| **Company details** | |
| Poshbags4rent www.poshbags4rent.de | Poshbags4rent is headquartered in Eschborn near Frankfurt am Main, Germany. |
| **Company's industry** | Rental of luxury bags |
| **Country of origin** | Germany |
| **Dimensions** | |
| **Product dimension** | The products are luxury designer purses and handbags from companies such as Luis Vuitton, Bogner, Aigner, Gucci, Prada, Versace and Chanel. These purses are cleaned after they are sent back to the company. |
| **Service dimension** | The service is the rental of the purses. Users that register with the company pay a monthly fee for a membership. Depending on how long the purse is rented, an additional payment has to be made. However, it is also possible to rent the purses as a guest for a higher price. |
| **Other links** | |
| **Other Crucial Dimensions** | |
| **Hybrid orientation** | User Oriented |
| **Community as service** | No |
| **Target market** | B2C |
| **Revenue model** | Monthly payment, pay as you consume |

**Images**

Product dimension

Service Dimension

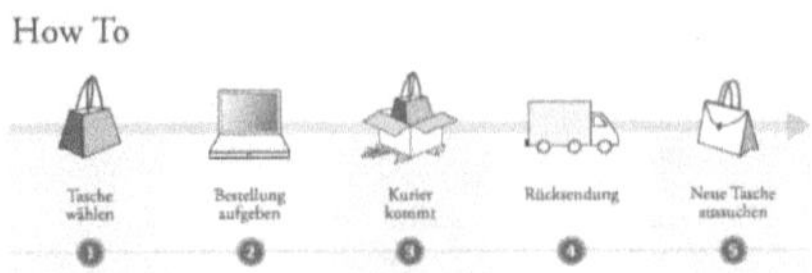


Information Systems I - Innovation & Value Creation
Friedrich-Alexander University Erlangen-Nuremberg
Lange Gasse 20, 90403 Nuremberg, Germany
www.wi1.uni-erlangen.de

Vivek K. Velamuri
Tel.: +49 (0)911 5302 152
vivek.velamuri@wiso.uni-erlangen.de
www.hybridvaluecreation.com

*Figure 24: Example of case PoshBags4Rent*

# Annex B: Interview Citations

## Part IV

## Empirical Study 2:

## The Cluster of Embedded Products

- "It is more difficult to solely distinguish on the basis of a product. It is the service component that really gives us the edge over our competition. We aim to be better in analyzing vital signs of our users… this should be our intellectual property"
- "We are a sports goods company and we are good at it. We don't want to develop software as we will only make a fool of ourselves".
- "… also we needed electronic hardware for our offering. We really don't have the competencies to produce or even work with such a product"
- "The e-book reader is a gateway to future revenues. Books on demand anytime and everywhere! This is how business will be".
- "… once people get comfortable with this technology they will really start appreciating the advantages of on-demand music. Instant delivery! No CD! No scratches! No space required to store your collection. And your whole collection is mobile".
- "Convenience is the key to success. It has to be very easy and simple to use the online shop in connection with the product".
- "… the service aspect is not elaborate enough. It is only an add-on to our core product".
- "We have never used a subscription revenue model. Hence it is something we are not used to".
- "… subscription is for newspapers and magazines, and it does not suit our business. This is too radical for our taste".
- "I can't ask my customer to buy an expensive gadget and then ask him to pay extra every month".
- "… a real service would be when, music is not purchased. But customers pay a monthly fee to have access to all the music that is available".
- "The success of our strategy is directly dependent on how well our online shop is integrated in the whole offer".

- "The goal of making more revenues through selling more e-books directly depends on how the customers perceive our service offering in the form of the online store".
- "We could have provided the same trainer as an offline tool. But it was a very good decision to go for ASP (application service provider). Now with so much information we are in a position to really understand our customers".
- "We do see the benefits of building a community. We have been successful in building a film community and we want to replicate this. But it will be open to all people who read books. Not just e-books".
- "We are an engineering firm. Not an internet startup. But we know we want to build a community. All our competitors are building one. But it is not easy for us".
- "Our customers are unique. Playing with programmable toys as a hobby is not for everyone. So our community is an integral part of the offer as it brings together scattered users from all over the globe into contact with each other. They share, they juggle ideas. It adds tremendous value to our offering".
- "We are in discussion to open a call-center to cater to the specific needs of our embedded product users. We also want to inform ourselves how the customers use our embedded product. And what their expectations are".
- "... we use a marketing push strategy. The techies design and produce our products. They have no contact with our customers and limited contact with us".
- "... I am told what to sell. I am the one who comes in direct contact with customer. But I never have the chance to get in touch with the technical department. To be honest, I don't think they are really interested."

## Part V
## Empirical Study 3:
## The Cluster of Solutions

- "If a service can only thrive by itself when it is provided free, then probably the service has no value".
- "If the customer is willing to pay for it, only then you know that the particular service makes sense and should be persisted with".

- "… now then if you decide to give it for free anyway, that's another issue, that's ok. But the customer needs to appreciate the benevolence shown".
- "Uptime services are in many cases too futuristic for our customers. Hence we let them (customers) decide to what extent they sign up for such service contracts. In many cases customers decide to be more adventurous as time passes and opt for guaranteed outcomes in a long run".
- "The main service is uptime service. We provide the customer about 90% of availability. We say within maximum ten hours knock down the machine runs again. We guarantee a sort of patient throughput. We guarantee that you can treat at least for example twenty patients a day. That is what we guarantee. Failure is expensive for us as we have to then pay financial penalties".
- "… most do not understand the numbers behind the success of a service organization. Ten preventive maintenance visits cost less than one machine failure".
- "Cleaning is an art and a science. It is a profession. It is not something everyone can do but it can be taught systematically in classroom. And once we realized the potential we started a cleaning academy".
- "We do some leasing, but to be honest, we don't do a lot because it's not attractive for us. This is really not our competency. Saying this, we rather work with 3rd parties who provide the required financial solution. Be it loans or leasing contracts. Something we ourselves do, if we are required to providing a leasing contract".
- "… the company philosophy is that all should benefit from breakthroughs in medical technology. We finance well, it is our competitive advantage".
- "… for example, with the help of usage statistics and experience you can optimize the temperature at which you want to wash or compress the length of wash programs, while still maintaining or improving quality standards".
- "Considerable cost saving can be realized by optimizing washing programs".
- "There is a lot of potential as technology moves forward. The machines can communicate back to you and tell you things, tell you how many chemicals they used, how much they worked and where the problems are. You can identify faults before they cause any work disruption".
- "… another option is of course to use indoor GPS, you could track the machines and you could provide a history of what they have done. This information could be very valuable. Especially, as customers outsource cleaning to a contractor

they want to monitor the contractor. The contractors find it attractive as they can not only monitor their employees but also provide proof to their clients of their work".

FSC
www.fsc.org
MIX
Papier | Fördert gute Waldnutzung
FSC® C083411

Kolibri 360 GmbH
Ferdinand-Jühlke-Straße 7
99095 Erfurt, Deutschland
produktsicherheit@kolibri360.de